In *Obviously, I'm Not from Here,* Dr. Veronica Lac doesn't just talk about multiculturalism, social justice, and equine therapy, she invites you into a conversation and a different experience. Daringly personal, Dr. Lac's vulnerability and openness invites the reader to engage on a deeper level and explore one's own experience with challenging topics. This book does a remarkable job at disarming while probing and recognizing challenges while offering hope for a path forward. Already recognized as a leader in equine psychotherapy and learning, Dr. Lac continues her trailblazing by moving into new, sometimes hostile, territory with balance, sensitivity, and compassion. Practical, touching, and challenging, this is a must read for all professionals in equine facilitated psychotherapy and learning.

Dr. Louis Hoffman, Executive Director, Rocky Mountain Humanistic Counseling & Psychological Association. Fellow, American Psychological Association (Divisions 1, 10, 32, 36, 48, 52)

I0128528

A West Africa proverb brought to attention by novelist Chinua Achebe notes, "Until the lion tells the story, the hunter will always be a hero." In this brave and personal telling, Dr. Veronica Lac becomes the lion, sharing her experiences of cultural difference and not-belonging as a British Chinese woman transplanted to the United States. In challenging her own attitudes, stereotypes, and biases, she grants us the grace to concede the encultured, unconscious beliefs and judgements that feed our own prejudicial blind spots. This is not a "how-to with horses," although many equine individuals are present and respected throughout. It is rather a clear call out as to why diversity, equity, and inclusion matter and what we can all begin to do about it. This book invites readers on a journey of self-discovery that is in no way simple or without unsettling emotion—and, oh my, is it worth it!

Gala Argent, PhD, Human-Animal Studies Program Director,
Animals & Society Institute and co-editor of the book,
*The Relational Horse: How Frameworks of Communication, Care,
Politics and Power Reveal and Conceal Equine Selves*

Anyone who seeks to understand how to center diversity, equity, and inclusion in their life and participate in the systemic change that is needed will benefit from reading this book. Dr. Veronica Lac writes with knowledge, clarity, authenticity, and vulnerability. Wherever you are on your journey in understanding the importance of DEI, this book will provide support, guidance, and important questions to consider.

Kathy Alm, CEO, PATH International

In her book, Veronica writes, "The ripple has started," and her words flow forth with exactly what the equine assisted services industry and beyond need to hear. The question of whether we are ready for it no longer matters because the future of our industry is here. This book hits hard and hits home from the beginning and offers tangible steps to facilitate braver conversations about diversity and equality. She recognizes differences in a way that considers an individual's autonomy and moves beyond thinking of dualistic concepts of "right and wrong" to a place of acceptance and respect. The emphasis on collaboration and connection in the industry of equine assisted services is a call to arms for those willing to accept it. I am a loud yes!

Dr. Cheryl Meola, LCMHCS, NCC, Founder, Mane Source Counseling

A true resource for understanding belonging, diversity, equity, and inclusion in services that include equine interactions. Part reflection, part education, this book is full of examples that help bring awareness into action for a more just future.

Nina Ekholm Fry, Director of Equine Programs, Institute for Human-Animal Connection, University of Denver

With humbleness and grace, Dr. Lac, drawing from her personal experiences as a British, Chinese American, artfully describes the importance of incorporating cultural awareness and sensitivity into equine facilitated psychotherapy and learning. Capitalizing from her decades of experience as a certified therapeutic riding instructor and Founder/Executive Director of The HERD Institute, Dr. Lac walks readers through numerous critically important factors to consider when conducting equine facilitated work as a culturally competent facilitator. This unique book, through a series of engaging, thought-provoking chapters, encourages practitioners to look within, question preconceived assumptions, and intentionally create inclusive, inviting spaces when conducting equine facilitated work.

Dr. Lori Kogan, Professor of Clinical Sciences, College of Veterinary Medicine & Biomedical Sciences, Colorado State University. Human-Animal Interaction Section Chair, American Psychological Association, and Editor of *Human-Animal Interaction Journal*

Wow! I sat down and devoured this book in a day. Each section was educational, deeply enriching, and challenging. I especially enjoyed sinking into the somatic experience of having "BRAVER Conversations" around Diversity, Equity, and Inclusion (DEI) in the equine facilitated psychotherapy and learning world. Case studies illuminate how DEI can show up in sessions, and what it truly means to "bake" DEI into an equine facilitated program. I was also humbled by the authenticity and honesty from all the contributors. An absolute must-read! Thank you, Veronica, for this book!

Shannon Knapp, Founder/President, Horse Sense of The Carolinas Inc.

Obviously, I'm Not from Here

Embodying a Sense of Belonging with the Help of Horses

by Veronica Lac, PhD

University
PROFESSORS PRESS

Colorado Springs, CO
www.universityprofessorspress.com

Copyright © 2023 Veronica Lac

Obviously, I'm Not from Here: Embodying a Sense of Belonging with the Help of Horses
By Veronica Lac

All rights reserved. No portion of this book may be reproduced by any process or technique without the express written consent of the publishers.

ISBN (Hardcover): 978-1-955737-38-8
ISBN (Paperback): 978-1-955737-39-5
ISBN (Ebook):   978-1-955737-40-1

University Professors Press
Colorado Springs, CO
www.universityprofessorspress.com

Cover Image by Veronica Lac
Cover Design by Laura Ross

Dedication

For Alfie, our golden boy, who started me on my journey home, and whose presence was our home. Forever missed and forever felt.

Table of Contents

Acknowledgments

They say it takes a village to raise a child. I don't have human children, but I do believe that birthing a book is not a solo venture either. I'm grateful for all the human and non-human animals who have been part of my journey for this book. Although I started writing this in 2017, this journey began from my earliest memories. In a way, this book is who I am, and the village that raised me included some incredible people.

I would not be who I am without the encouragement of my husband, Quan. Thank you for your love, patience, and unwavering support in seeing my sensitive soul as my strength, and for believing in me when I doubt myself. Most important, I am grateful for your willingness to step into the unknown with me, embracing the adventures that come our way. Knowing that we can love, laugh, live, and grieve together at every turn allows me to spread my wings and guides me home.

I am blessed to be able to call my colleagues my friends. This book would not have been possible without my HERD team members attending to the daily operations of the institute while I disappear into the abyss of my writing for weeks. When folks ask me how I find the time to write a book while running a business and managing a farm, I tell them it's because I've surrounded myself with the most amazing people: Rachael Loucks, Diana Bezdedeanu, and Katie Wheeler have been instrumental in implementing our vision of collaboration and community at The HERD. My deepest appreciation to you all for all that you do to keep me on track. Sarah Morehouse, your unwavering loyalty and support means the world to me. I'm so proud of how far we've come and so grateful that you have walked with me every step of the way in the last five years. Elizabeth McCorvey, I offer you my utter devotion! Your mentorship and friendship have revolutionized my sense of who I am in relation to the world we live in. Your rebel instinct is contagious, and I am dedicated to basking in your joyful presence. Thank you for holding space for all of who I am. And, to Mira Gruber, I am eternally indebted to you for the loving care that you offer our HERD ponies, pups, and chick chicks, so that I can rest and recuperate.

What I've enjoyed the most about this book is being able to invite chapter contributions from a few of our HERD faculty members, students, and graduates to showcase the work that they're doing in their communities. Dr. Kelsey Dayle John, Yoshi Babcock, Catherine Manakas, Elizabeth McCorvey, Rachael Loucks, Ellen Lichtenstein, Danielle Mills, and Naomi Nyamodoku have all bravely shared their experiences. I am humbled by your courage and trust in me through this process. Writing this book and developing The Inclusive HERD™ program has also offered me some delightful connections with other Black, Indigenous, and People of Color (BIPOC), and allies who are aligned with our vision and mission of increasing accessibility, diversity, and inclusion in the equine-facilitated space. I am deeply humbled by our growing connections and want to offer my gratitude to Nahshon Cook, Abriana Johnson, Michael Kaufmann, Miyako Kinoshita, Nina Ekholm Fry, and Kathy Alm for leaning in so I know I'm not alone in fighting this fight.

My heart fills with love and gratitude as I think of each and every single student, graduate, and instructor who has joined the HERD programs. With every iteration of the curricula, and every time I teach, I learn something new. I am so proud of the community that we are building together, and thankful for how each member of the HERD shows up to support each other. I am truly humbled by their talents and their passion for what they bring to the communities they serve.

Finally, I am beyond grateful for all the animals in my life that inspire me to do this work. To our dog, Tyson, whose aging body reminds me that time is precious, encouraging me to slow down and be present with him, I offer my continued devotion. To our pandemic pup, Gracie, I promise to chase away the storms. To my equine herds, past and present, I profess my heartfelt gratitude: Rupert, Reba, Cheyenne, Arrow, Infinity, Ernie, Rocky, Will, Philippe, and so many more; I thank them all for leading me home.

Preface

"Warning: do not read this if you don't want to engage in a discussion on human rights. Do not read this if you don't want to hear the voice of a person of color. Do not read this if you are comfortable with the status quo. Do not read this if you are too exhausted and feel that the world is condemning all white people.

Please note: If you are able to choose not to read this because of the warnings above, then you are lucky that you have the choice not to face this every day, and I would encourage you to come back and read it at another time. Because you need to."[1]

On June 4, 2020, I published a blog piece on The HERD Institute® website with the disclaimer above. At that time, the world had been at a standstill due to the COVID-19 pandemic, and people were just beginning to re-emerge from the shelter-at-home orders that were put in place to mitigate the spread of this new and deadly virus. Here, in the United States, tempers were already flaring in protest against the lockdown. And while white men with automatic rifles had protested on the steps of state capital buildings across the country with immunity only a few days before, the peaceful protests of Black communities in protest of the murder of George Floyd had brought the riot police out in full force.

Around the world, organizations suddenly woke up to the need to address racism and began releasing anti-racist statements and promoting Black, Indigenous, and people of color. Anti-racist virtual book clubs began popping up specifically for white folks to study the work of authors such as Ijeoma Olou (*So You Want to Talk About Race*),[2] Austin Channing Brown (*I'm Still Here: Black Dignity in a World Made*

---

[1] Lac, V. (2020). Resilience, recovery, and reconnection. HERD Institute. Retrieved from https://herdinstitute.com/resilience-recovery-and-reconnection/

[2] Olou, I. (2018). *So you want to talk about race.* Seal Press.

for Whiteness),[3] Ibram X. Kendi (How to Be an Anti-Racist),[4] Layla F. Saad (Me and White Supremacy),[5] Resmaa Menakem (My Grandmother's Hands),[6] Robin DiAngelo (White Fragility: Why it's so Hard for White People to Talk about Racism),[7] and others. It felt like many individuals were opening their eyes to the need for these uncomfortable conversations and wanted to do their part to dismantle centuries old prejudices and hateful rhetoric.

And yet, for those of us who exist in marginalized groups, there was a collective gasp—a mixture of relief, cynicism, fear, and hope: relief that this time had finally come; cynicism about the legitimacy and/or performative actions that some were taking; fear of retribution and heightened vigilance; and a microscopic sliver of hope that perhaps, finally, this uprising would lead to lasting change. We knew that the murder of George Floyd was a symptom of a broken society and that the root cause of his death, and the deaths of many others like him, ran deep and wide. These symptoms manifested in micro and macro levels and were nuanced and multi-faceted.

Within the equine industry, those of us who identified as Black, Indigenous, and people of color, were aware that members of the various equine related organizations that were putting out anti-racist statements may not be on board with the premise of the need for anti-racist measures that their leadership teams were promoting, and that many people were reacting in anger to the terms "privilege" and "white fragility," as well as increasingly defiant about being racist at all. I wanted to raise awareness of this within our community of equine-facilitated practitioners and challenge some of these positions.

In the blog post, I wrote:

> It's been an exceptionally tough week. In the midst of the global pandemic, the witnessing of yet another incident of police brutality has ignited a firestorm of reactions around the world. The death of George Floyd was a horrific example of

[3] Brown, A. C. (2018). I'm still here: Black dignity in a world made for whiteness. Convergent Books.
[4] Kendi, I. X. (2019). How to be an antiracist. One World.
[5] Saad, L. F. (2020). Me and white supremacy: Combat racism, change the world, and become a good ancestor. Sourcebooks.
[6] Menakem, R. (2017). My grandmother's hands: Racialized trauma and the pathway to mending our hearts and bodies. Central Recovery Press.
[7] DiAngelo, R. (2018). White fragility: Why it's so hard for white people to talk about racism. Beacon Press.

institutionalized racism. But let's not forget the equally disturbing and calculated racism aimed at Christian Cooper when a white woman banked on the knowledge that she could weaponize this institutionalized racism.[8] The insidiousness of that incident somehow leaves me feeling more spooked than the blatant disregard for humanity for George Floyd. Let me be clear, I'm not saying that what happened to Christian Cooper was worse, only that it affected me differently.

Since moving to the States almost a decade ago, I have lived in three different states and experienced the vast differences in regional attitudes and reactions when people meet me. As a British Chinese woman who drives a truck, listens to country music, and works with horses, I'm aware that I'm a bit of an anomaly. My expectation and experience of blatant racism follows me from a lifetime of living in predominantly white spaces. What does it say about our society that it never surprises me when I hear about the institutionalized racism that Black and Brown communities experience every day? That people of color have been brought up to expect to be treated with such disregard? What does it mean to you that in some ways I'm more comfortable with knowing that, because at least we know what we're dealing with and what to look out for?

But what Christian Cooper was met with chills me to the bone. The worst kind of racism comes from those who don't think that they are racist. It comes from folks who think they are color blind, or folks who think they don't have biases. As part of The HERD Institute® certification programs, students are introduced to Project Implicit, a pioneering force behind challenging attitudes, stereotypes, and hidden biases that impact the way we perceive others. By partnering with Harvard University, they have created online assessment tools to highlight areas of implicit bias. The assessments they offer are free, and I highly recommend you take a look if you haven't come across them before. What always surprises me is when students enter into our training believing that they don't hold any biases, or when doing the assessments admit to trying to give the "correct answers," or those who react

---

[8] Christian Cooper, a Black man, calmly asked a white woman to leash her dog in Central Park in New York City, as per park regulations. She responded by calling police and telling Cooper "I'm going to tell them there's an African American man threatening my life."

defensively against the results given by criticizing the format of the tests. I'm not saying that the test designs are critique proof, but the interesting thing for me in how folks respond to them is the underlying idea that if we hold any biases at all, it means that we are not evolved enough as human beings, so we have to defend ourselves from that notion and aim to be completely bias free.

I am a person of color, and I am racist. I am sexist. I am homophobic. I am politically incorrect. In short, I am prejudiced and biased and have been complicit in the oppression for those who I stand in solidarity with in so many ways. Why? Because I live in a society that has conditioned me to be that way. Institutionalized racism, heteronormativity, ableism, misogyny, colonialism, and patriarchy have shaped me by osmosis, and continue to influence me through the media and my lived experiences in everyday life. While I make every effort to be mindful of some deeply embedded prejudices, fight for equality and equanimity, and stand alongside all who are misrepresented and oppressed, I know that I will always have my blind spots. I say all this, as a person of color, to alert my well-intentioned white friends that it is okay to acknowledge our inherent biases and privilege. What we do with the awareness of these is more important than spending our energy being defensive and denying their existence.

Taking a stand against bigotry and hate requires us all to examine our own prejudice. It's uncomfortable, and often deeply unsettling, to admit to the judgments that we hold. The act of being an ally begins with working through these ourselves, before we even enter into the dialogue. Within the current political climate, it is imperative for us all to take action, speak with compassion, be clear in our intention, and acknowledge that prejudice resides in us all. In doing so, we can step away from the defensiveness that arises when someone points out our privilege. Somehow, in the current discourse, the term privilege evokes anger and denial, as if admitting to having privilege in any way makes us a bad person. If that has been your understanding, let me be clear: having privilege doesn't mean it's your fault that people are oppressed, but denying that you are privileged makes you part of the problem. This isn't a process of privilege shaming; it's an opportunity to reflect on what we have been blessed with and find compassion for those who are less fortunate. Privilege

*shows up in a multitude of ways, every day, and allows us to seek
to understand the experiences of those without.*

*The aim is not to erase all of our biases but, instead, for us to
acknowledge that we all have unconscious biases, and that we
need to work to raise our awareness of them. By bringing these
biases to light, we can actively choose, and reflect on, our
thoughts and actions from a different lens. We ALL have biases as
a result of being alive in a relational space; our environment, our
culture, our upbringing, our experiences, and our own choices
speak volumes about how we have become who we are. Stepping
into an equine-facilitated setting with the intention to be aware
of our biases so that we can interact with our participants and
horses with intentional non-judgment helps us to provide a safer
space for all.*

I started writing this book in 2017, way before the global pandemic
and the protests for racial justice. And yet, despite the time lapse, the
message I want to deliver has not changed. Rather, it is now even more
relevant. I couldn't have known how the murder of George Floyd would
mobilize so many to stand up for those who have been oppressed. I
couldn't have known how the global pandemic would elicit the empathy
of the privileged to feel the existential crisis and fear for their bodily
safety that many Black, Indigenous, and people of color face every day.
Now, more than ever before, I am witnessing friends, colleagues, and
students grappling with their own implicit biases and taking
accountability for the ways that they have unconsciously been
complicit in the oppression of others. This is hard, heart-wrenching,
and humbling work that requires all of us to dig deep and find
compassion and empathy to carry us through the discomfort.

While I feel that this is progress in many ways, there is much more
work to be done, particularly within the equine industry and the
equine-facilitated field in which we are situated. As the Founder and
Executive Director of The HERD Institute®, I am committed to
increasing diversity, equity, and inclusion within this field and teach
from a framework of cultural competence. Diversity training isn't
something to be completed in one module but seen as part and parcel
of the continuing developments of relational ethics requiring constant
reflection, infused through all that we do.

While my blog post spoke about the importance of recognizing our
unconscious biases, I also want to recognize the intersectionality of
privilege and oppression. I may have experienced sexism and racism in

my life, but I am also privileged by being a cis-gender, heterosexual woman without physical or cognitive disabilities. I have lived an economically privileged life that has afforded me housing, healthcare, food, relative financial security, and the means to access the highest levels of education. Some of these advantages I've worked hard for, but for the most part I was born into them. Having these privileges does not mean that I am actively oppressing others. What I do with this awareness is what's important. Denying that I have them limits my ability to find empathy for those who are struggling. Using my voice from a place of privilege and creating opportunities for others to step up can help to empower those who are disenfranchised.

You may be wondering how any of this is relevant and why I'm even sharing it with you. Well, in my worldview, all organizations begin with the vision of their leaders, who realize their visions from the context of their lived experiences and personal values. My experiences of not belonging have meant that I have worked hard to cultivate a culture of inclusivity within the HERD Community.

In writing this book, my aim is to shine a light on how the socioeconomic structures that have been established within the societies in which we live are naturally a part of the fabric of the equine-facilitated industry that we have all co-created. I want to promote a culture within our community of diversity, equity, and inclusion, operating from a spirit of abundance. This is written into our mission statement at The HERD Institute®. I want to live by these values. I also want to hold hope that it's possible to champion others who are different from ourselves, to hold the belief that there isn't just one way, and that within our field of equine-facilitated work, we are all, individually and collectively, ultimately working toward the same thing: healing and growth in the communities and organizations that we belong to and serve.

This book is for anyone working within the equine industry who wants to gain a deeper understanding of what it means to be inclusive. It's for equine-facilitated practitioners working with clients in marginalized populations who need to become more culturally attuned to those they serve. It's for people who are struggling with a polarized political climate and feel that there is nowhere safe for them to turn— white folks who feel under attack, angry, and misunderstood; Black, Indigenous, and people of color who feel angry, exhausted, and overwhelmed; and LGBTQIA individuals whose civil and human rights are being threatened in many parts of the world. I want to share my experiences as someone who is also struggling with how to acknowledge my blind spots and offer a framework to bridge the gaps and mend the ruptures that have opened up in people's lives.

I want to promote dialogue and curiosity, uncover the more shadowy parts of our industry, moving away from dogma, ruptures, and denial to a more robust, resilient, and relational space. Perhaps by starting small within one organization, we can create a ripple effect into the life space that we all occupy within and outside of our industry. But let's not be naïve. This book comes with the warning that it may cause discomfort and ruffle some feathers.

My wish is that we can find ways to bolster our resilience as we grapple with these issues, look for opportunities to lift one another up as we recover from the collective trauma of the global pandemic while acknowledging the racial inequalities it has highlighted, and in doing so reconnect with ourselves and one another.

I'm doing it because I believe in hope. I hope that we can come together as a community and address the disparities within our field. I hope that we can build bridges toward increasing diversity and inclusion so that all our voices can be heard. My hope is that by doing this those who have felt invisible can feel seen, and those who have felt marginalized can feel worthy of belonging. Because you are. You belong. Here, in the HERD, and in the world. I see you and you matter. I hope that you will join me in this quest and in doing so find ways to offer a sense of belonging to all who enter this space.

With hope,
Dr. Veronica Lac

Foreword

The irony is not lost on me that I am writing the foreword of a book about embodying belonging while 5,000+ miles away from my home on a fast train through the UK countryside (which happens to be Veronica's home). It's serendipitous really, much like my introduction to The HERD Institute and practitioners in the equine-facilitated learning space. I have been within six degrees of separation from Dr. Veronica Lac for quite some time.

As I listen to the conversations of passengers on this train, conversations between my team of facilitators (three American, one Scottish, and one English) I can't help, but smile. We don't belong here necessarily, but we have created a sense of belonging together through our leadership development work with horses. Our passion, dedication, and future in equine-facilitated learning come from our own lived experiences with horses. This shared experience has created a sense of belonging amongst us, much like Veronica describes in this book.

I was introduced to The HERD Institute and Veronica while conducting market research for a brand management client. I was searching for high-touch/intimate equine-facilitated practitioner training programs that deliver a quality framework while building an impactful community. Through this research, I found another good friend, Elizabeth McCorvey, who also contributed to this book. Although psychotherapy was not the specific practice I had in mind, I quickly recognized Veronica as a creator with a story—someone who learned a system, saw flaws in the system, and dedicated her career to making safer, more intentional practices. Research aside, I had to send her a Facebook friend request because she is the kind of person I enjoy surrounding myself with.

As a Black horsewoman with a background in veterinary medicine, there were few places I felt like I belonged. As a Black woman in the horse industry, it took a balance of appreciating my own Black cowgirl culture and longing for more before I found a community I felt comfortable in. As long as I remember, any time I have felt resistance or uninvited to a table, I made it my goal to create a whole new table that welcomed people who aligned with my values. From my podcast to my children's books and my career, I have committed to being a creator and noticing when there is a community or connection that needs building.

The nuance behind the word "belonging" is so delicate, and I truly respect its exploration in this book. Where can I exist while connected to others, being all of who I am, loving, and being loved freely? This book delivers several key DEI-related challenges through personal anecdotes with academic references to explain how to hold space for difficult conversations and create impactful change in the horse industry. You will experience the processing of Veronica's own experiences, which lend incredible insight about how marginalized groups navigate the world, and you will hear from members of her HERD who have experienced their own inequities in the equestrian space. It is truly a gift to hear these different perspectives. I hope you digest them and think about what it means to reckon with the discomfort their experiences may bring to you.

This book challenged me to self-reflect: How can I look critically at my experiences and develop an awareness of how they impact my body, my decision making, and my growth? If you have trouble sitting in discomfort, know that you are not alone. When I reached the chapters related to white privilege, inequity, and how to have braver conversations, I realized I have the tendency to zoom out or skim the passage, especially when the topics hit close to home. This happened twice before I realized the pattern. I had to go back and ease my way into managing my discomfort.

If you are not prepared to do this inner work, know that you can read this book more than once and gain a new perspective every time. Veronica creates a capsule of psychological safety that allows you to explore the root of your own thinking and gives you tips on how to move through any roadblocks that may occur.

I encourage you to not only read this book yourself, but to share it with someone within your horse community. Did you notice I didn't say "Share it with another marginalized horse person" or "Share it with the one non-white rider at your barn"? It is so important to understand that DEI conversations are not just for marginalized groups. Share this book with someone who would benefit from a new perspective, one who could shift their behaviors to create better spaces for everyone in the horse industry.

Thank you, Veronica, for your vulnerability and your willingness to advance this industry past the rivers and the lakes that we are used to. Thank you to every contributor whose story leads to a deeper understanding of how versatile the horse industry is and can be. Also, a big thanks to you for reading this. May you be inspired by what you learn here and lead the way toward a more inclusive future for our industry.

To the sound of hoofbeats,
Abriana Johnson

Part I:

Longing for Belonging

Chapter 1

Belonging

A deep sense of love and belonging is an irreducible need of all people. We are biologically, cognitively, physically, and spiritually wired to love, to be loved, and to belong. When those needs are not met, we don't function as we were meant to. We break. We fall apart. We numb. We ache. We hurt others. We get sick.
~ Brené Brown[1]

> Where do you belong? How do you know you belong? I'm not asking you where you're from, but where do you feel with the whole of your being that sense of connection to yourself and others, where you can be all of who you are and know that you can love with abandon and be loved just as you are? Is there a physical place that you can close your eyes and picture to bring that feeling into your body? Or is it a person, animal, a smell, a texture, a taste that can transport you to that sense of belonging? Are you one of the lucky ones that can answer these questions easily? Or has it been a life-long struggle to find that feeling? Does it happen upon you fleetingly and then is lost in the wind?

Coming Home

Where do you feel at home? Say the word out loud right now. Home. What happens in your body as you say the word? Home. For me, when I say "home," I experience the word bodily as a deep exhale. I recognize this exhale as both an embodied memory of safety and well-being and

---

[1] Brown, B. (2010). *The gifts of imperfection: Let go of who you think you're supposed to be and embrace who you are.* Hazelden Publishing.

a yearning for something that is often out of reach. Of course, your response to saying the word will bring up something unique to you at this moment. Your response may also depend on where you are right now as you read this. If you're physically located in a place where you feel at home, you may react differently than if you're in an unfamiliar setting. As someone who has lived in multiple countries, states, and cities, I have become adept at living the adage of "wherever I lay my hat, is my home" in a practical sense. But home is both a place of abode and something much, much deeper in my bodily experience.

Think about the last time you moved. Whether it was to a new house just minutes away from where you previously lived or across town, state, or county lines, or an international relocation. What was the first thing you did upon arrival at your new residence? What did you keep with you as you moved? As you re-oriented yourself to the new space, what comparisons did you make to where you moved from? How long did it take you to feel settled and for it to feel like home?

There are many of us who experience a sense of displacement after a physical relocation. Military families move, on average, every two to three years. This means that for a military child, it's not uncommon to have moved schools 6–8 times between kindergarten and high school graduation. Many professions and industries also require frequent relocations: doctors, veterinarians, oil and gas, aerospace, and academia, to name a few. For those of us who have lived this relatively nomadic life, we have learned the skills to attempt to create a sense of home and community wherever we land, often in locations not of our choosing. Navigating a new environment (climate, geography, ecology), culture, language, and people becomes part of everyday life.

I remember when we first moved to the United States, I spent the first few days relying on our GPS to navigate us from our temporary accommodation to wherever I needed to go. This was back in the day when GPS navigation was relatively new and would regularly lose connection, so I'd find myself driving along only to suddenly be disconnected and literally have no idea where I was relative to where I needed to be. I quickly realized that I needed an embodied sense of where I was and bought an old-school road map of the local area and stuck it on the wall. Immediately, I felt more settled in my body.

Research suggests that finding places that feel like home can contribute to overall health and wellness. A sense of home is intricately linked with a sense of belonging. Sociologist Vanessa May distinguishes between sensory belonging and relational belonging.[2]

Sensory belonging encompasses the need to feel anchored geographically. Our attachment to physical places is embedded by sensory experiences. We become familiar with the sounds in our home late at night; listening to the rhythms of our environment helps to alert us to danger when we hear something unexpected. Our sense of smell is intricately linked to our parasympathetic nervous system; it's the basis of aromatherapy and offers a gateway to deeply rooted memories. Sensory belonging also explains why my immediate need upon arriving in the States was to locate both the British aisle at the local supermarket and my nearest Asian market. May states that "The foods we grow up with look, smell, and taste familiar and are an important source of cultural belonging" and that food provides a sense of home. Studies in immigrant experiences of adapting to their new country indicates that homesickness (the longing for home) is triggered by memories evoked from sights, sounds, smells, and tastes. This sensory, embodied experience becomes integrated as an undercurrent of their new world.

I resonate with this process in my attunement to hearing different languages and accents. I always feel comforted by hearing someone speaking in an English accent in the United States; my ears are so attuned to the need to find the familiar. Similarly, my search for an Asian market was realized one day as I was walking around Walmart. I felt a surge of excitement when I heard a woman clearly reprimanding her child in Cantonese a few aisles over from where I was. Using her voice as a beacon of hope, I hurried through the store in search of her. I'm not sure what her experience was of this slightly manic Chinese woman descending upon her.

"Excuse me, I'm sorry to trouble you. I'm new to the area, and I was hoping you'd be able to give me some recommendations for good Chinese markets and restaurants here." I said in Cantonese. "Aiyah!" she exclaimed, "You poor thing. Here, let me give you some places." With that, she started digging into her purse and pulled out a Ziplock bag. I'd somehow encountered a perfect stranger who had a penchant for collecting business cards from local Asian restaurants. "Here," she said, "this is the best place for dim sum, this one is good for seafood, this is the best hot pot, and this one for noodles." She beamed at me, clearly thrilled that she was able to help me find a sense of home and put her

2 May, V. (2011). Self, belonging and social change. *Sociology, 45*(3), 363–378. https://doi.org/10.1177/0038038511399624

collection of business cards to good use. Then, in broken English, she said to me "Go find, happy. Eat!" With that, she bustled off after her child who had wandered down the aisle.

I never knew her name and we never met again, but when I recall that exchange I can still feel the sense of warmth, gratitude, and welcoming embrace that this encounter provided me in that moment. Through that interaction, my sense of feeling lost in a foreign land, untethered, unstable, and estranged from all that was familiar evaporated for a moment. It is precisely that feeling of being fully seen while taking the risk to ask for support that I hope to offer others in community spaces.

Chapter 2

A Part of, Apart From

In South Africa, a common greeting is sawa bona, which translates to "I see you" or "I acknowledge your existence." The response to this greeting is sikhoma, which means "I am here – when you see me, you bring me into existence." The more I think about it, the more it feels as though in every space I enter, I am waiting for someone to exchange this pleasantry with, not just in word but in intention. And usually, I am met with silence.
~ Jessica J. Williams[1]

Existential psychologist James Bugental talks about the experience of being human as that of being a part of all others while being apart from.[2] The feeling of being alone in a sea of people is both liberating and terrifying; the freedom to be who you are authentically is always juxtaposed with the need to belong. This universal struggle of existential isolation is exacerbated for folks from historically marginalized populations. Our need for attachment and belonging is a survival instinct, so when faced with the choice of speaking our truth at the risk of isolation, because what needs to be said goes against the grain of majority standards or perspectives, it's natural to opt for silence and belonging.

When I first arrived in the USA, I reveled in the All-American tradition of Thanksgiving. I loved the idea that this was a holiday dedicated to our ability to feel gratitude rather than one of commercial gifts and gains. I felt humbled by the spirit of abundance and generosity extended by our new friends in our newly adopted homeland and the

---

[1] Williams, J.J. (2021) Black surrender within the ivory tower. In Burke, T., & Brown, B. (eds). *You are your best thing: Vulnerability, shame resilience, and the Black experience— an anthology* (p. 173). Random House.
[2] Bugental, J. F. T. (1999). *Psychotherapy isn't what you think: Bringing the psychotherapeutic engagement into the living moment.* Zeig, Tucker.

sense of inclusiveness I experienced. Many times over the past few years, as my husband traveled for work, I was home alone for Thanksgiving and was invited to join my friends with their families on the day. Tables were extended, and I had found a welcoming place to land.

In the decade since my first American Thanksgiving, I have come to understand that this is just one version of this holiday. As my network of friends and acquaintances has grown, I have been introduced to the real story of thanksgiving from an Indigenous people's perspective: a story of colonization and brutality toward the Wamponoag people. I have felt shame at my ignorance and a responsibility to acknowledge the full picture.

And yet, I still feel pulled toward celebrating Thanksgiving in the "traditional" way with a day of feasting, family, and friends, all focusing on what we are grateful for. Each year, I battle this cognitive dissonance and struggle to balance myth with the truth: join in the festivities or honor those who mourn? I've rationalized that it's possible to be respectful of those whose historical trauma is triggered by these annual festivities while also holding gratitude for the abundance before me. I've succumbed to the pleasures of the day while telling myself that it's not "my" history and, therefore, not my loss to grieve, and subsequently felt the shame of that. I've tried to appease my guilt by volunteering at homeless shelters every year before indulging in the abundance.

What I'm aware of in all of this is my fear of ostracizing myself if I were to voice these struggles. Of course, I've been thankful for the inclusive opportunity to celebrate with others, so if I were to mention the real story of Thanksgiving, would I be offending those who are celebrating? If I don't, am I part of the collusion to eradicate an important part of history that needs to be brought to light for it not to be repeated?

I work with many organizations that struggle with conflict management. I have found that beneath the issues and concerns is this same fear: Will I be isolated if I speak up? Whether we are working with organizations, in education, or with individual therapy clients, we are still attending to human needs and desires for belonging. I saw a meme I "liked" recently on social media that said something about how we can disagree and still love one another. A couple of minutes later, I saw another one that challenged this perspective, with the added comment of "unless your disagreement is rooted in my oppression and denial of my humanity and right to exist." I caught my breath as I read that, and "liked" it, too. Therein lies my biggest fear. How can I speak up without risking isolation? Can I trust that if I disagree with you, you'll love me anyway? And if your truth fundamentally denies my right to exist, where do we go from there?

When we talk about belonging, it's easy to mistake it with identity. Belonging refers to an internal sense of safety, acceptance, and inclusion. Feelings of belonging are supported by shared beliefs, values, experiences, and sense of identity. The relational belonging that May describes includes attachments to people, animals, land, and structures. Identity refers to an individual's attributes, characteristics, or personality that is either self-claimed or externally ascribed. For example, I can claim that I am an Asian American by virtue of being a Chinese woman with US citizenship, but I don't necessarily belong in a group of other Asian American women since I don't share the same experiences as Asian women who were born in the US, and who have a commonality of experiences that are unique to that group. However, externally, you may see an Asian woman and assume that I belong to that group by ascribing to me the identity of an Asian American.

This nuanced process of internal/external identification to groups is something that we play out continuously in our daily lives with ourselves and others. It's a primal part of being human, a necessary survival instinct, to categorize and label what is friend or foe. Zoe Lieberman and her colleagues conducted research to show that this ability to distinguish between social categories is already embedded by the time we are in infancy.[3] This instinctive ability to discern shared attributes is then reinforced by the process of self-identification and affinity toward sameness, leading people "to be partial to members of their own group (ingroup) relative to those from other groups (outgroups) in terms of social preferences, empathic responding, and resource distribution." Lieberman and colleagues state that some of the unintentional but inevitably undesirable effects of this process of social categorization result from "the biased belief systems that social categorization supports—including stereotypes for, essentialist beliefs about, and even dehumanization of members of certain social groups."

This is, in essence, implicit bias. And yet, these two words are increasingly becoming censored as a result of the polarized political climate in the United States. There is a growing political movement to

---

[3] Liberman, Z., Woodward, A. L., & Kinzler, K. D. (2017). The Origins of Social Categorization. *Trends in Cognitive Sciences, 21*(7), 556–568. https://doi.org/10.1016/j.tics.2017.04.004

expressly ban such conversations around diversity, equity, and inclusion.

In April 2022, Governor Ron DeSantis signed into Florida law a bill that he called the "Stop WOKE Act," otherwise known as Florida House Bill 7/Senate Bill 148 (HB7).[4] This bill seeks to "Stop the Wrongs to Our Kids and Employees (W.O.K.E.)" by banning corporate training and school, college, and university curricula that make employees and students feel "uncomfortable" about the actions of their ancestors through teaching the tenets of Critical Race Theory (CRT). Proponents of the bill seek to eradicate discussion of CRT, believing that it is inherently divisive and discriminatory. The bill extends the right of employees to sue their employers for discrimination under the Florida Civil Rights Act if the employer violates the statute by talking about these topics in the workplace in any subjective way that supports "indoctrination" of these ideologies. This means that the act prevents employers from mandating any diversity training that includes any of the prohibited concepts. HB7 of the Florida Civil Rights Act now states:

> ...that subjecting a person, as a condition of employment, membership, certification, licensing, credentialing, or passing an examination, to training, instruction, or any other required activity that espouses, promotes, advances, inculcates, or compels such individual to believe any of the following concepts constitutes discrimination based on race, color, sex, or national origin under the Florida Civil Rights Act:
> 1. Members of one race, color, sex, or national origin are morally superior to members of another race, color, sex, or national origin.
> 2. An individual, by virtue of his or her race, color, sex, or national origin, is inherently racist, sexist, or oppressive, whether consciously or unconsciously.
> 3. An individual's moral character or status as either privileged or oppressed is necessarily determined by his or her race, color, sex, or national origin.
> 4. Members of one race, color, sex, or national origin cannot and should not attempt to treat others without respect to race, color, sex, or national origin.

---

[4] Florida Senate (2022, March 3) CS HB/7: Individual Freedom. Retrieved from https://www.flsenate.gov/Session/Bill/2022/7/BillText/er/PDF

5. An individual, by virtue of his or her race, color, sex, or national origin, bears responsibility for, or should be discriminated against or receive adverse treatment because of, actions committed in the past by other members of the same race, color, sex, or national origin.

6. An individual, by virtue of his or her race, color, sex, or national origin, should be discriminated against or receive adverse treatment to achieve diversity, equity, or inclusion.

7. An individual, by virtue of his or her race, color, sex, or national origin, bears personal responsibility for and must feel guilt, anguish, or other forms of psychological distress because of actions, in which the individual played no part, committed in the past by other members of the same race, color, sex, or national origin.

8. Such virtues as merit, excellence, hard work, fairness, neutrality, objectivity, and racial colorblindness are racist or sexist, or were created by members of a particular race, color, sex, or national origin to oppress members of another race, color, sex, or national origin."

> Let's take a moment right now to breathe and check in with your body. How does the wording in this bill land with you? What are you feeling in terms of physical sensations? How's your breathing?

When I first read the excerpt of the HB7 bill above, I noticed tension in my jaw and a tightening in my belly. I also noticed that the more I read, the more I clenched my jaw and my breath became shallower. I happen to live in Florida, so this legislation has real implications for me as an educator and an employer. This law is designed to further exclude and erase the experiences of marginalized groups and prevents educators and businesses from offering space for important conversations. The success of this legislation isn't necessarily in the number of actual lawsuits filed. The impact is already apparent in the way educators and businesses are canceling courses on racism or offering training on diversity and inclusion.

This isn't the only legislation in Florida that restricts educators in discussing issues that attempt to increase diversity, equity, and inclusion. In May 2022, DeSantis also signed into law the so-called "Don't Say Gay" bill, which prohibits classroom instruction on sexual orientation or gender identity from kindergarten through 3rd grade, or in a manner that is not age appropriate for students, to prevent indoctrination. This was swiftly amended in April 2023 to expand the prohibition to *all* grades with additional legislation to make it a felony to provide gender-affirming healthcare to transgender minors. The impact of this bill is being felt by teachers and students throughout Florida, with reports of censorship of lesbian, gay, bi-sexual, transgender, queer, intersex, and asexual (LGBTQIA) students protesting the bills, with schools being mandated to remove children's books depicting same-sex relationships (e.g., *Purim the Superhero*, by Elisabeth Kushner, a picture book about a Jewish boy with two dads), and limiting teachers to talking about families only in the context of heterosexual relationships.

In these legislations, what stands out is the use of the word "indoctrination" and the fear of the development of a critical consciousness in young minds and the public at large. The tragic consequences of these laws are the further psychological harm inflicted on those who are already at a higher risk for depression, anxiety, self-harm, and suicide. These bills make it not just acceptable but *mandatory* to erase the experiences and existence of marginalized individuals, further exacerbating feelings of isolation in LGBTQIA and Black, Indigenous and youth of color individuals by fundamentally challenging their right to exist.

Take a breath. Notice your bodily response. What do you agree with? What do you want to push away? Breathe and bring to mind a place where you feel safe and hold that in your body.

Chapter 3

Crucial Conversations

The truth is, we live in a society where the color of your skin still says a lot about your prognosis for success in life...ignoring race will not change that. We have a real problem of racial inequity and injustice in our society, and we cannot wish it away. We have to tackle this problem with real action, and we will not know what needs to be done if we are not willing to talk about it.
~ Iljeoma Oluo[1]

We are hard-wired to search for safety, affinity, and belonging through what is familiar and alike. Which means that for us to embrace difference, unfamiliarity, and the unknown, we are going against what has been embedded in us since infancy. It means that it takes conscious effort, intention, and awareness to understand how to be inclusive of others who are not like us. Which means that it can be hard to navigate and requires commitment and humility to know that we might not have all the answers, that we will make mistakes, and that it is a continuous journey of discovery and not a set destination.

But why is talking about diversity, equity, and inclusion so hard? What is it about the words *racism, racist, homophobia, transphobia, supremacy, fragility, privilege, oppression, prejudice,* and *power* that trigger so much emotion in all of us? Notice what happens for you right now even reading those words. How are you experiencing the meaning behind those words? Perhaps you're noticing the edges of anger creeping in, or the faint touch of shame or guilt, or fear, uncertainty, and anxiety, or maybe indignation. Maybe you have a sinking feeling in your gut, or the urge to sigh, or perhaps a sense of helplessness, exhaustion, or grief.

---

[1] Olou, I. (2018). *So you want to talk about race.* Seal Press.

Whatever you become aware of, allow yourself to feel it. These feelings are valid and important in this journey of self-discovery. It's the beginning of excavating our instinctive and habitual responses so that we can become more aware of how we might engage in these crucial conversations differently. Whether you occupy a position as part of the dominant culture in your daily existence or hold the experiences as part of the historically marginalized, or find yourself existing in both arenas, our emotional responses to conversations about diversity, equity, and inclusion will always be borne from feelings of vulnerability. Take a breath. Notice your bodily response. What do you agree with? What do you want to push away? Breathe and bring to mind a place where you feel safe and hold that in your body.

Research indicates that conversations about diversity, equity, and inclusion, particularly when primarily focused on issues of race, racism, privilege, and systemic oppression, often result in heated exchanges. This may stem from fears of offending, feeling judged, or being misunderstood. There is often confusion and/or anxiety as folks grapple with the multitude of definitions and terminologies, which may exacerbate feelings of powerlessness and despair. Many people are overwhelmed by their feelings of shame, guilt, anger, or indignation.

Social researcher Brené Brown, highlights the different strategies we use to defend ourselves against vulnerability (and potential shame): We can go on the attack, we can run away, or we can appease.[2] This is similar to how all animals, humans and non-humans, might react to a traumatic event or a threat to our survival: fight, flight, freeze, or fawn. Each of these are instinctive responses in an effort to protect oneself from harm and are so embedded in our biological repertoire that it often happens without apparent warning or awareness. This process is referred to as an amygdala hijack, a term coined by Daniel Goleman,

---

[2] Brown, B. (2012). *Daring greatly: How the courage to be vulnerable transforms the way we live, love, parent, and lead.* Avery, p. 145.

where we respond to an external emotional stimulus as if it were a physical threat.[3]

If we take a step back for a moment and think about this in the context of systemic racism and white supremacy, it becomes clear that the heightened emotions that folks experience during these difficult conversations are very real. These words and concepts are heavily loaded for those who have power *and* those who experience marginalization. There is an inherent threat to the status quo within those concepts that is often met with defiance, denial, and retaliation, which can lead to actual physical threats on those calling for social justice. This was exemplified in the case of the McCluskeys, the wealthy white couple in St. Louis who felt the need to point an AR-15 rifle and a handgun at Black Lives Matter protesters marching through their neighborhood. I have no doubt that they both felt physically threatened in that moment by what they experienced as an "angry mob" trespassing on private property; yet there was no evidence of violence or physical threats from the protestors toward them that warranted this response.

Whether or not you agree with the McCloskeys' actions, we cannot get away from the reality that the discourse on social policies and social justice, not to mention gun legislation, have life-threatening consequences. We need to find a different way to engage with these topics without escalating a conversation toward an amygdala hijack. In his book *The Polarized Mind*, Kirk Schneider says that psychological polarization is the process of subscribing to one point of view to the utter exclusion of any alternative, and that polarization tends to be based on fear.[4] This fear is real and embodied in every fiber of our being, activated as a traumatic response to anything we instinctively perceive as potentially dangerous.

Resmaa Menakem, in his book, *My Grandmother's Hands,* explains,

> The body is where we live. It's where we fear, hope, and react. It's where we constrict and relax. And what the body most cares about are safety and survival...from the body's viewpoint, safety and danger are neither situational nor based on cognitive

---

[3] Goleman, D. (2007). *Emotional intelligence* (10th ed.). Bantam Books.
[4] Schneider, K. J. (2013) *The polarized mind: Why it's killing us and what we can do about it.* University Professors Press.

feelings. Rather, they are physical, visceral sensations. The body either has a sense of safety or it doesn't.[5]

Additionally, he suggests that

> When one settled body encounters another, this can create a deeper settling of both bodies. But when one unsettled body encounters another, the unsettledness tends to compound in both bodies. In large groups, this compounding effect can turn a peaceful crowd into an angry mob.[6]

A settled body is one that is fully present, mindful, calm, and attuned to the environment, with a regulated nervous system, bringing an energetic quality that fosters well-being and healthy engagement with the world. An unsettled body is one that is experiencing some level of dysregulation in the nervous system, bringing an energetic quality that invites chaos and a sense of being overwhelmed that is more likely to lead to an amygdala hijack. For those of us who work with children, dogs, and horses, we are witness to this process every day. How often have we experienced our horses getting spooked more readily when we are feeling unsettled or nervous ourselves?

When a settled body encounters an unsettled body, we can lend our settled body to help co-regulate the unsettled body. Our dog, Gracie, is terrified of thunderstorms. In fact, she's terrified of a lot of things. We adopted her at the height of the pandemic at a year old. Gracie is a cattle dog-Weimaraner-bluetick coonhound mix, full of energy and zest for life—that is, until she gets scared. We've learned that she's scared of thunderstorms, gunshots, fireworks, sudden movements, her own shadow, and she once was spooked by a leaf blowing in the wind. When Gracie gets scared, her response goes from zero to being overwhelmed in a matter of seconds. She tucks her tail and looks for a safe place to hide. And then she shakes and trembles until the threat is over.

Initially, when she got overwhelmed, my husband and I would attempt to soothe her, stroke her gently, and let her know she's okay. With hindsight, I recognize that in those moments, I was also unsettled. I wanted her to be okay and felt powerless to help. No matter what we

---

[5] Menakem, R. (2017). *My grandmother's hands: Racialized trauma and the pathway to mending our hearts and bodies.* Central Recovery Press, p. 39.
[6] Menakem, R. (2017). *My grandmother's hands: Racialized trauma and the pathway to mending our hearts and bodies.* Central Recovery Press, p. 39.

tried (deep pressure massage, CBD treats, wrapping her in blankets and a Thundershirt), nothing worked. After a while, instead of running to hide, she decided that the best solution would be to climb into my lap. This soon became problematic given that I live in Florida and thunderstorms are a daily occurrence!

It didn't matter if I was in the middle of a Zoom meeting, Gracie would haul her 45-pound frame into my lap and sit on me, blocking my view of the computer screen and amusing whomever I was in session with, panting and drooling on my shoulder in an ever-increasing state of agitation. If I pushed her off, she would simply insist on climbing back up. Again, I can now see that in those moments, I was unsettled. I wanted to make sure that she was okay, but my attention was also on ensuring that my Zoom session wasn't interrupted. I'd feel irritated and helpless.

This cycle continued for a while until I took Gracie to an assessment with a dog trainer. After talking through our aims for Gracie, we sat down on a couple of couches across from each other in his training room. As Gracie walked toward him, we heard the rumble of an approaching storm. Immediately, she ran towards him and attempted to climb into his lap. He asked me what I would normally do in this situation and laughed out loud when I told him. He invited me to observe his response.

Taking a deep breath and exhaling, he gently but firmly asked Gracie to get off. She tried to climb back up and he offered her some space next to him. All the while, he continued talking to me calmly, explaining that he wasn't going to reinforce the idea that there was something to be afraid of. He simply offered her his presence as a settled body. Gracie lay down next to him and stopped shaking.

Inwardly, I was mortified! *I know this stuff!* I know how to co-regulate with my clients and my horses. I know how to settle babies (I'm really rather good at getting them to sleep), and yet I'd somehow missed the connection with Gracie.

I relay this story to emphasize that it doesn't matter how much we know in *theory*, unless we put it into *practice* we will continue to repeat patterns of behavior and ways of interacting with others, *especially when we are unsettled*. Barbara Rector, known to many of us as a predecessor in our equine-facilitated industry, talks about the importance of bringing intentional attention to our relationships in each moment. She explains that this is the process of not only seeing something but being clear about your intention in how and why you are looking at it to begin with, and how with that intentional attention it is then possible to find a way forward in a co-created, collaborative way. I knew that what I was seeing was my dog in distress and I was looking for ways to solve the "problem," but I hadn't stepped into connecting with her intentionally to pay enough attention to what she actually needed from me in those moments. She didn't "need" to sit on my lap. She needed me to help her find regulation. She needed me to be settled in my body so that she could settle, too., so that she could feel safe.

It seems then, that our task in the context of understanding diversity, equity, and inclusion is to find ways to engage in these difficult, crucial conversations from an embodied sense of safety. This requires us to learn strategies to physically, emotionally, and cognitively calm our nervous systems before, during, and after these discussions.

In the following chapters, we'll be exploring some of these strategies, regularly returning throughout the book to awareness exercises to practice, embed, and embody feelings of being settled so that we can move toward embodying a sense of belonging for ourselves while creating the capacity to support others to do the same.

My hope is that these stories will offer a different perspective of what diversity, equity, and inclusion mean in the context of the work that we do as equine-facilitated practitioners, while highlighting the importance of creating an intentionally inclusive space for those we serve. This will not be an easy book to read. It's certainly not been an easy book to write.

Recently, I was asked in an interview why I am committed to centering diversity, equity, and inclusion in my work. My motivation stems from knowing what it feels like to not be in the ingroup, always looking in as an outsider, to not see others like me in the spaces I occupy and in the experiences where my presence is perpetually being questioned implicitly, and explicitly. In short, my embodied, lived experience is one of longing to belong. I am beyond grateful to have learned the skills to cultivate an embodied sense of belonging for myself and our HERD community, and I want to extend that to our wider community and to those we serve.

Chapter 4

You Had Me at First Sniff

"Slow down! Make him slow down!"
"No! This is FUN!"

The sun glimmered through the forest canopy and the gentle breeze accentuated the gloriously unmistakable smell of the horses. I recognized the smell from when I had stuck my face into a pony's mane at a petting zoo. Walking up to the stables, I was barely able to contain my excitement. We were on a family vacation at Yosemite National Park. I was seven years old, and I was finally old enough to ride off lead on a trail ride. I remember the breeze on my face as we rode along the forest trail, and the flea-bitten grey pony I was on, diligently following nose to tail behind the horse in front. Most of all, I remember my brother's cries behind me as the horses began to trot, and his pleas for me to slow my pony down. Meanwhile, I was delighting in the sensation of speed and abandonment. That moment changed me forever.

I've often wondered whether I would have been as daring on that pony if it were not for my brother's fear. Was I proving that I could be braver than he was, or did the thrill of the ride capture my imagination? Either way, although I didn't know it at the time, that moment was the beginning of my journey towards a life with horses.

Up until the age of nine, I lived on the 11th floor of a pet-free high rise in the concrete jungle of Hong Kong. The closest I got to horses was at petting zoos. Yet even in those early years, I longed for their solid presence and was fascinated by books that featured horse and human adventures. I had wild daydreams of working on a dude ranch in Montana or Wyoming, of galloping across the North Yorkshire Moors, and of days filled with barn chores and sharing apples with my very own pony. I spent hours in daydreams and imaginative play, turning the bamboo cane that threatened us from atop the cupboard into a friendly hobby horse, galloping up and down the tiny hallway in our apartment. In one way or another, horses were a part of my life.

When I was twelve, I met my soul-sister-best-friend-forever at school. We bonded over our joint obsession with all things pony (real and imaginary). Lisa grew up with real horses and was already an accomplished rider. I lived vicariously through her equine adventures and soaked up her lived experiences as though they were my own. She regaled me with tales of riding through the desert in Egypt, of galloping along the beach in Cyprus, and of sitting atop her first pony practically before she could walk. It all sounded so romantic and liberating to my city dweller mind. Since that trail ride through Yosemite, I had begged my parents at each and every opportunity to go horseback riding whenever we went on vacation, so they finally caved and enrolled me in a handful of riding lessons around this time.

My memories of these lessons consist of bleak, damp, winter evenings at the stables, having confusing directions shouted at me by my instructor, with me engaged in a battle of wills with a Shetland pony named Peter Blue. I was in a group lesson with three other girls, all of whom were older and taller than I, so I was assigned the smallest pony. I was also the only first-timer in the group, and Peter Blue was deemed to be a beginner's ride, an added reason that I was paired with him. Enter my first experience of a love–hate relationship.

Looking back, I'm sure that Peter Blue was most likely an overworked, old-school riding pony who had been treated as a commodity all his life. I feel a twinge of guilt and sadness now as I recognize his behaviors as signs of stress and soreness. Back then, my 12-year-old self didn't know any better and simply attempted to follow instructions to "give him a good old pony club kick" to get him moving. He would move but only to stop short again after a few strides, turn toward the gate, and refuse to budge. I was told that I wasn't being firm enough with him and that I needed to kick harder. When this produced no forward movement, my instructor would come up behind us and slap him hard on the butt to get him going. Needless to say, this routine was repeated throughout the lesson. After about four weeks of feeling demoralized by my lack of confidence and a sense that I really didn't want to beat the poor pony with a stick each time I got on him, I decided that perhaps riding wasn't for me after all and gave up. Although I couldn't articulate it at the time, this traditional approach to learning to ride just didn't fit with my way of being in the world. It would be a long while before I returned to being on horseback on a regular basis.

Still, my love affair of all things equine continued. Lisa and I would sneak off to the stables in our free time to visit our favorite horses. We started volunteering in the local therapeutic riding center. We'd bring apples and carrots and stick our noses in the horses' manes and breathe deeply. Even then I knew how therapeutic that was and how much I needed it. Somehow, deep in my soul, I had already registered my first lesson from the horses: Be here now and breathe.

Reflection Questions

How did you come to love being with horses? What do you resonate with in this story? What do you *not* recognize from your experiences? What surprised you?

Chapter 5

In My Blood

Given my city dwelling childhood and its corresponding deprivation of connecting with nature and animals, my affinity for horses was always a bit of a mystery to me. If you'd asked me what it was about horses that drew me to them, I wouldn't have been able to explain it other than to say that I felt at home with them.

A few years after my grandpa died, I was visiting my grandma and came across some old photo albums hidden away in the back of the cabinets in my uncle's office. The albums at the front of the pile contained hilarious, and often embarrassing, photographs of my brother and me from our childhood. Sporting fabulous outfits of flared corduroys, flowered shirts, and denim overalls, they depicted a privileged upbringing of trips abroad to Hawaii, Japan, Australia, England, and the United States. What struck me in these albums was the look on my face whenever I was pictured with any animal: the koala bear at Brisbane Zoo, the tiny rock python I held in the palm of my hand, the Alaskan Huskies on a dog-sledding experience, and, of course, the multiple trail ponies wherever we went; my joy and awe from each experience shone through. And although my expression is different in it, I would also like to include the photo of me with the inanimate seahorse from Ocean Park in Hong Kong that I was most adamant in riding. The pout was a result of being told to dismount. A seahorse is still a horse, right? (See Picture 1).

I also noticed that the rest of my immediate family was never pictured with an animal. My mother had severe allergies, and my brother wasn't even comfortable with dogs, so I guess it made sense that he wouldn't want to hold a snake; but it still struck me as a little odd. My dad grew up with cats but would never acquiesce to my pleas for a kitten. Where did my fascination with animals come from? As I continued to dig through the old photo albums, I began to unearth some precious gems. The further back I reached into the cabinet, the older the photographs. I discovered my parents' wedding album, and then pictures of my mother and my uncle as children. There were black and white photos of my grandma, beautiful and elegant in her traditional Chinese *cheongsam* dresses, carefree holiday snapshots, family gatherings of somber-looking men and women, and a treasured photograph of my grandparents on their wedding day.

I kept digging further into the cabinet and stumbled across a worn, hardback book with a faded embossed title on the front. Brushing off the dust, I attempted to decipher the script. My level of reading in Chinese is elementary at best (although I have some proficiency in reading menus in Chinese restaurants; I mean, I have my priorities!), but I managed to figure out that it was some kind of yearbook from 1936 entitled "27 months in training." Flicking through the pages, I was stopped in my tracks by pictures of horses and gun carriages, cavalry soldiers and their mounts, and picture collages of a day in the life of a young cavalryman in training. My heart ached as I realized that these were pictures from my grandpa's training camp at military school in Japan. Tears welled in my eyes as I gently turned the pages, and then suddenly, there he was: Grandpa, on an enormous thoroughbred, clearing what looked like a five -foot jump.

I was crying, not only because I wished that my Grandpa was still alive so that he could tell me about his experience, but because I realized that he had done so many years ago, but I had been too impatient to listen to an old man's tales. I was crying for the young soldiers in the yearbook, and the majestic steeds they rode, and I was crying because I knew that the story did not end well for so many of them.

This was 1936. My grandpa's graduation certificate attached to the yearbook indicated he had spent just over two years in training with his Japanese brethren. Less than a year later, he was back in China in the Nationalist Army heading into war in the Sino-Japanese conflict, facing hand-to-hand combat against his training buddies. In subsequent photographs within my treasure trove, I discovered pictures of him in full army regalia, standing proud alongside his war horse. I cried some more. At last, I had come across "proof" that horses were in my blood. Mixed with the feelings of awe and horror for the young men pictured in the yearbook was a sense of connection to my heritage.

Throughout history, the horse has been integral in China's development. From as early as the Shang Dynasty (c. 1600–1100 BC), horses were viewed as essential partners in the human quest for survival. They were regarded as noble creatures that were worthy of companionship in the afterlife and were often entombed with their owners for this purpose. The Chinese Empire was vast and full of conflict, but at one time stretched from the steppes of Mongolia down to the South China Sea and across Central Asia. During the Shang Dynasty, the Bronze Age was already well underway within the Empire, written language was developing, and military strength and aristocratic privilege were shown through the number of horses and chariots one owned. Horses were also inextricably part of the communications, transport, and farming infrastructure of the country.

By the time of the Han Dynasty (c. 206 BC), the Emperor was particularly struck by the majesty and endurance of horses from the Ferghana region of Central Asia, the imports of which eventually established the trade routes of the famous Silk Road. The Ferghana horses were known as the "Heavenly Horses" and linked to the mythical role of the horse within Chinese culture, belief in the ability of horses to transport their riders to the "home of the immortals." Chinese legend holds that the horse and the dragon are closely related—specifically, the *longma,* a mythological creature represented by a horse covered in dragon scales. The symbolism of heavenly horses and *longma* are evident in Chinese art, poetry, and language, so much so that woven into classical Chinese literature, the *longma* also became an idiom for an eminent person, or one with vigorous spirit, and is often used in a phrase to wish longevity for another at birthdays and celebrations.

Of course, the mythical history of the horse is not unique to Chinese history, and this is not a book about the evolution of Chinese horsemanship. I digress as a pondering on how my way of being in the world is always against a backdrop of my culture and my assimilation (or not) of my heritage as I learn new skills and absorb new knowledge. This duality of being comes to the forefront most often when I become aware of my difference to those around me. Having spent my whole life attempting to blend in so that those differences aren't so apparent, I am sometimes taken aback when I am faced with the obvious.

The joy in finding my grandpa's yearbook was quickly followed by a heart-stopping question: What if everything I know about horses comes from a white man's perspective?

As a British Chinese woman, I have never encountered anyone else in the horse world that shares my heritage. The majority of my horse experience had been guided by white male figures, whether on the ground or in the saddle at clinics, workshops, and lessons. My mind began racing with questions: What might my Chinese culture teach me about being with horses? Does being Chinese explain some of the struggles I'd had in the way I'd been taught to be with them? Are horses different in different cultures? Can I be truly authentic with my horse if I don't acknowledge my culture?

This was a stunning realization for me, but it was also strangely familiar. It reminded me of times during my training as a mental health practitioner of being aware of my cultural difference, and yet feeling the need to swallow teachings that didn't fit with my worldview. As part of my graduate program in Gestalt Psychotherapy in England, we were required to have a minimum of forty hours of personal therapy per year in the modality of our training during the four-year program. I tried in vain to find a Chinese Gestalt therapist and discovered that the only licensed one at that time lived in Australia. Since this was well before telehealth was available, I had no choice but to work with a therapist who was ethnically different from me. As it turned out, in my quest to find a Chinese therapist, I befriended the only other two Chinese Gestalt trainees in England, Mae and Billy. The three of us quickly established a peer group to support ourselves in our training journey, meeting over dim sum and noodles in Chinatowns around the country, sharing our understanding of how Gestalt theories could be integrated into Chinese culture, and generally geeking out. These peer group sessions solidified my awareness of the yearning within me to assimilate ideas and concepts through a cultural lens. Now, years later, I faced the same process with my understanding of horsemanship. Once again, I was faced with a lack of a role model.

> **Reflection Questions**
>
> What resonated with you? What was unfamiliar to you? Who have your role models been? How did you find them? How much effort did it take to find them?

Chapter 6

Even the Rat Was White [1]

If you are not represented, then your story does not exist. If the people constructing your narrative do not reflect the diversity of this world, then your story is not your own.
~ Shannon Walker, Founder:
Social Disruption [2]

Representation matters. If you've been fortunate enough to grow up in an environment where you can see people who look like you being represented in the world around you and in the media, then it may not have even occurred to you that others are under-represented. After all, as the saying goes, a fish doesn't know what water is. In the same way, I don't generally spend my days thinking about whether I can breathe— unless my ability to do so is being compromised. Research has shown that children's early experiences shape what they can imagine is possible. [3] Providing role models that kids can relate to in terms of gender, religion, race, sexuality, physical abilities and size, and neurodiversity is a critical part of supporting identity development and cultivating feelings of belonging.

---

[1] *Even the Rat Was White* by Robert V. Guthrie is a historical review of psychology that exposes the history of racism ideologies within psychology that has been used to legitimize the dehumanization of African Americans and promote ideas of Black inferiority. Guthrie, R. V. (2004). *Even the rat was white: A historical view of psychology* (2nd ed.). Pearson Education.

[2] Walker, S. (n.d.) *Social disruption.* Retrieved from
https://www.socialdisruption.co.uk/about

[3] Abdullah, M. (2019, April 30). Five childhood experiences that lead to a more purposeful life. *Greater Good Magazine.* Retrieved from
https://greatergood.berkeley.edu/article/item/five_childhood_experiences_that_lead_to_a_more_purposeful_life

I was incredibly privileged in my upbringing in many ways in having clear role models in my life that affirmed my belief that barriers were set to be broken. I was brought up listening to stories of the women in my lineage who had gone against the grain. My grandmother was a trailblazer who embodied a sense of quiet revolution, pushing the boundaries of the cultural norms that she was born into. As the youngest of nine siblings, Grandma was lucky to have been born at a time where the painful tradition of feet binding was falling out of fashion in China, while her eldest sister had to endure the lifelong agony of walking on broken and maladapted feet. At a time when women rarely worked outside the home, Grandma worked for a civil engineering firm that designed and constructed the first flyover in Hong Kong. She'd been inspired to challenge gender stereotypes by one of her sisters who had been one of the first female doctors trained in the United States to return to offer Western medicine in China.

It wasn't just the women in my family who were unafraid of stepping into the unknown. I grew up listening to stories of how my great-great-grandfather was part of the influx of Chinese laborers during the California Gold Rush in the 1850s. I grew up hearing about my dad's humble beginnings in Malaysia, living in a house on stilts above the river where he could fish out of his bedroom window. He was devoted to rescuing stray cats that slept with him under the mosquito net and spent his childhood running barefoot through the Sabah sugar cane fields. These stories instilled in me the belief that anything is possible and the value of dreaming big, as well as providing me with a place to retreat to internally when my external world was at odds with these beliefs.

The homogeneous environment of predominantly white faces that I encountered at school was a painful contrast to these empowering stories. I was one of only a few Chinese students at my school in England for the first few years of my attendance. While we may have naturally gravitated toward one another, we had been told in no uncertain terms that congregating in this way would be frowned upon, and speaking in Chinese was forbidden as we were there to "assimilate and integrate." Naturally, I didn't pay too much attention to the rules and would regularly hang out with one other Chinese girl. While we never spoke in Chinese when we were together, our report cards would always include comments of the need for "further integration." Our teachers would deliberately keep us apart during class group activities by assigning us to different teams.

To this day, I'm not sure what the motive behind that was other than to reinforce the notion that "white is right" and any deviation from the majority culture was, well, exactly that—deviant. It would have made more sense to me if either of us had been struggling with learning the language, but we were both fluent in English and spoke without any hint of Chinese accent, socialized with others in our peer group, and were steeped in the UK pop culture of our generation. Our weekly highlights included watching Blue Peter every afternoon, Top of the Pops on Thursday nights, and the A-Team and Knight Rider on Saturday mornings. Chinese New Year went by uncelebrated, as did the Lantern and Mid-Autumn festivals. And yet, somehow, that still wasn't enough. It felt like the mere fact that we wanted to be in each other's company caused the powers that be some discomfort. I guess there was fear in the unknown.

This attitude wasn't reserved only for Chinese students. I remember distinctly when we were told that two new girls were joining us part way through the academic year. This was in the mid-1980s during the height of the Ethiopian famine, after the Live Aid concert had captured the hearts of many to fundraise for the plight of starving children. So, when our principal took great pains to explain to us that the girls were from Ethiopia, there was an audible gasp across the auditorium. We were explicitly told to "treat them as one of us," which clearly meant that we were to ignore any differences they might present with. This didn't stop the rumor mill from churning out stories that the girls "must be orphans" and that they must have only been able to attend the school because of a generous scholarship program. The assumptions reverberated loudly through the hallways where colonial attitudes reigned. As it turned out, the sisters were from an affluent family with diplomatic ties to the UK and far from the image of starving orphans that everyone had conjured. Not long after their arrival, one of them pulled me aside and asked, "Why is everyone so wary of us?" I had no answer for her but took this as an invitation for friendship and a sign that she felt safe enough with me in my being different to ask that question.

I felt a sense of freedom in my friendship with these girls that I didn't with some of my white friends. My curiosity about their culture was reciprocated by their interest in mine. We were able to talk about our struggles and frustrations about being multicultural in a way that was met with acceptance that this was our reality, rather than with judgment of not being enough—not English enough, not Ethiopian enough, not Chinese enough. We were able to embrace our cultural differences, acknowledge what we missed from our respective cultural homes, and make fun of one another's cultural idiosyncrasies.

I remember thinking that my English friends didn't know what they were missing. Because many of them didn't. How could they embrace differences if they were told to ignore them or, worse still, actively dismiss them? With no awareness of how things might be done differently, how could my peers possibly be inclusive? Without the encouragement by our role models to be curious about differences, what chance did we have of finding belonging?

Reflection Questions

How many of your friends are Black, Indigenous, or people of color? How much do you know about their culture and cultural influences? How many of your friends identify as part of the LGBTQIA community? How much do you know about the leading voices in their community? How many of your friends were born outside of your native country? How much do you know about where they feel is home? When was the last time someone made you feel included? What helped to foster that feeling?

Chapter 7

Obviously, I'm Not From Here

I was bilingual in Cantonese (a Chinese dialect spoken by those in Hong Kong and Guangzhou province in China) and English by the time I was three years old. Growing up under the last vestiges of British colonialism in Hong Kong cultivated a deeply embodied sense of split loyalties in me from a very young age. My father was an up-and-coming lawyer who was making a name for himself, which increasingly afforded him access to a place at the table of the privileged few. I knew that many of the places we frequented had previously been establishments reserved for the English expats living in the colony to the exclusion of Chinese locals. The plush interiors of the Hong Kong Jockey Club, the Yacht Club, and the Hong Kong Country Club were decorated with portraits of white men in suits looking sternly down at us. I'm not sure if I was told that we were lucky to be there, or whether it was a sense of indebtedness that I picked up from the social elite that owned these spaces. I do remember being taught specific English table manners that were counter to Chinese culture and feeling anxious about the need to get it right in the presence of my English friends. It was clear that I needed to minimize the Chinese parts of myself in these environments.

At home, there was a stark contrast to these English spaces within the walls of our 11th floor apartment. I was surrounded by Chinese rosewood and mahogany furniture with its intricately carved dragons and phoenix motifs, and our walls were adorned with Chinese calligraphy and traditional scrolls, some of which were painted by my grandmother. We took pride in celebrating the mid-autumn festival with moon cake and honored the Chinese New Year with lucky red packets, glutinous rice cake, and sugared lotus seeds. My parents insisted that we speak in Cantonese at home, and since I attended an English school for regular classes, I also studied two hours every day after school with a Chinese tutor. The message that I received was that being Chinese was a source of pride—unless we were with white folks, at which point we must adopt a subservient position and defer to their rules of engagement.

In their quest to provide us with the best education they could afford, and in so doing emulate the British elite, my parents opted to send my brother and me to boarding school in England. After all, my father had completed law school in the UK and had fond memories of his time abroad. In preparation for this adventure, my dad gave me a boxed set of the Malory Towers books by popular British children's author Enid Blyton, full of stories about life at boarding school. Armed with the knowledge that my new school life would be full of midnight feasts, lacrosse, and endless slumber parties, I was so eager to depart for my new life that I barely registered the fact that I wouldn't see my family for months on end.

By the time I started school in the UK, a couple of months shy of my 10th birthday, I had been fully conditioned to the British stiff upper lip that would be expected of me on departure and had absorbed into my bones that all things British was best. I was well on my way toward dissociating myself from my Chinese culture, a process of internalized racism and colonialism that would take me decades to dismantle. In my second year of secondary school (translation: 7th grade), we were given an assignment in our English class to write our autobiography over the course of one semester. Entitled "Life goes on," my 12-year-old self wrote about the difficulties of fitting in and of being an outsider during my elementary school years as one of the few Chinese students in a predominantly white English elementary school in Hong Kong. Although I didn't have the words to elaborate on it then, I remember wondering about the irony of that situation, the power dynamics of colonialism, and the corresponding pursuit of Western ideals.

Part of the struggle for Black, Indigenous, and people of color living within predominantly white communities is finding a way to balance their internal sense of self and racial identity with the cultural norms they are immersed in. My experience within a colonial structure positioned all things British as the gold standard of how things should be, and yet within my family I was still expected to conform to the ideals of a traditional dutiful Chinese daughter. These dual expectations were often in conflict with each other, and therein lay my lifelong challenge: how to integrate, assimilate, and apply what I learn within the cultural context of my life without losing myself in the process. Derald Wing Sue, Professor of Psychology and Education at Columbia University and a leading scholar on multiculturalism, refers to this as acculturation: the process of social, psychological, and cultural change that occurs in the attempt to balance two cultures, leading to the inevitable adaptation to and adoption of the norms of the majority culture[1].

Fast forward a few decades. For the first time in my life, I am now identified as British first and Chinese second. This is a bizarre experience for me as I've spent the majority of my life trying to be seen as British, so I needed to adjust to this as my primary identifier. Here, in the United States, every time I open my mouth when I meet someone new, I am faced with the unmistakable look of confusion as whomever I am with visually experiences a sense of cognitive dissonance as they attempt to identify what/who I am. I realized pretty early on after we moved here that the best way to limit my audience's confusion is to declare my identity right off the bat. To that end, whenever I present at conferences, workshops, or training events, I have incorporated into my introduction this fact: "Obviously, I'm not from here."

What started as my need to retain my audience's attention by eliminating their need to guess or wonder about my origins, has turned into an embodied acceptance that this phrase has been accurate throughout my life. The fact is that wherever I am in the world, it is pretty safe to assume that there is no one else in the room that shares my diverse cultural heritage and experiences: as a Hong Kong-born, British-educated naturalized British citizen living in the United States turned US citizen equine-facilitated therapist/trainer, there is nowhere that I fully belong. Too Westernized for the Chinese community, not English enough for the Brits, and too British for the Americans. Throw in the equine-facilitated therapist thing, and I may as well say I'm from Mars.

That isn't to say that I haven't found ways to adapt to my environment. Nor am I saying that I haven't been welcomed into lots of different spaces. What it does mean is that I have learned to minimize my differences in various ways in order to not stand out. I have become very proficient at translating cultural differences in language and body movements. I've been doing it so long that it's second nature to change the "skin" I'm in and attempt to fit in, so much so that I sometimes forget that I'm doing it. It is a rare occurrence that I feel able to bring myself fully, with all of who I am, as I am, without translation into any encounter or space. I once wrote a paper for my doctoral program entitled "Shapeshifting: An Embodied Process Perspective in Transnational Psychology" to illustrate the nuances required to shift

---

[1] Sue, D. W. (2010). *Microaggressions in everyday life: Race, gender, and sexual orientation.* Wiley.

between cultures. I make the point that the shapeshifter offers a metaphor for a way of being for transnational individuals in how their embodied process adapts to and is impacted by their cultural embedment and immediate environment.

Think about traveling to a foreign country and how disorientating it can be. The sights, sounds, smells, spoken language (complete with differences in grammar and colloquialisms), body language (including differences in personal space and gestures), food, local customs and traditions, and not knowing the relative location of where you are to where you need to be can be overwhelming. A simple example was highlighted not long after moving to the States when I realized that I needed to relearn and adapt to which way to look before crossing the street. The challenge of navigating these cultural shifts fluidly, both internally and externally, is an ever present one for me.

The process of undoing decades of acculturation began during those peer group sessions with my fellow Chinese Gestalt therapy training colleagues and continues to this day. Recognizing how and when I defer to a colonial mindset, challenging and questioning my values and beliefs to uncover my own implicit biases, and embracing my differences rather than minimizing them is an ever-evolving process. Embracing my own differences is tough and comes with the risk of exclusion. It also brings the potential for the greatest gift. While living in Ohio, I was quick to realize that my Venn diagram of identity and belonging had very few intersections with those around me, so I had no choice but to embrace my differences and allow others to see me as such. In an ironic twist, I discovered that accepting I wouldn't fit in allowed me to be more authentic, which created a sense of belonging in the spaces that I occupied.

Brené Brown, social researcher and author of *Braving the Wilderness,* says that the opposite of belonging is fitting in, and that "true belonging only happens when we present our authentic, imperfect selves to the world."[2] One of my professors, Dr. Theopia Jackson, once said that the difficulty in being different is that there are very few places where one can find to fully exhale. We are hard-wired for connection, literally, in our neurobiological make-up, and this yearning for belonging and connection follows us through life. Some of us are lucky enough to have experienced these connections at a pre-verbal level, so that when we engage in relationships that resonate with

---

[2] Brown, B. (2015). *Daring greatly: How the courage to be vulnerable transforms the way we live, love, parent, and lead.* Avery.

us deeply, we have the embodied memory of what that feels like internally. We can recognize the potential of these relationships as they begin to emerge, cultivating them into fruition. For others, it is more difficult. When ruptures have occurred, or if these connections have not been present in developmental years, it is harder to embrace them when they appear later in life. Partnering with horses in the work we do allows people to experience this type of connection, which many of us yearn for. A space to be able to fully exhale. A space where we can meet one another in a place of authentic connection. A space where we can bring all of who we are and feel seen fully, without judgment. That's the type of space I hope we can create in the equine- facilitated world.

Reflection Questions

How many languages do you speak and/or have learned post formal education? Have you traveled internationally? If so, what was your embodied experience of being in different cultures? Where's the furthest you've been away from home (whatever home means to you)? How did you adapt to being in a different place? What was it like to return home?

Chapter 8

Staying Curious

Our only chance at dismantling racial injustice is being more curious about its origins than we are worried about our comfort.
~ Austin Channing Brown[1]

It's hardly surprising that these experiences in my formative years have led to a fascination for studying issues of diversity and inclusion and a commitment to influencing organizational strategies in these areas. Throughout my academic career, I have gravitated toward research in cross-cultural experiences. My undergraduate degree in public and social policy management culminated in a research thesis on cross-cultural adoption; my MA program in training & performance management led to a thesis on the importance of cultural competence frameworks for organizational development; my MA in Gestalt Psychotherapy concluded with a research dissertation on the experiences of clients of color working with white therapists. With hindsight, all these endeavors stemmed from a desire to shine a light on what were often difficult conversations that needed to take place within the context I was in. By the time I enrolled in my PhD psychology program, I was accustomed to these issues being swept under the carpet. So was thrilled when I met my mentor, Dr. Louis Hoffman, whose approach to international psychology was a breath of fresh air.

Dr. Hoffman was the first white psychologist I had met who actively encouraged us to critique mainstream psychology theories and concepts from our own cultural lens, whatever that might be. A prolific author, Dr. Hoffman has published multiple books and articles on existential–humanistic psychology and spearheaded the International Psychology Certificate program that formed part of my studies. Having spent the past decade liaising with Chinese scholars and organizing a

---

[1] Brown, A. C. (2018). *I'm still here: Black dignity in a world made for whiteness.* Convergent Books.

series of workshops and conferences in China, he was committed to working with students and clients through an indigenous psychology[2] perspective. He was quick to point out the cultural biases inherent in mainstream psychology theories, encouraging us to look beyond what we were learning by bringing in the cultural context of the work. So much of what I had learned was turned upside down and, in that process, shed some light on my own internalized "white is right" biases that I had not been aware of, which no doubt subsequently led to my a-a moment of questioning the Eurocentric approach to horsemanship that occurred a little later.

In contrast to my experiences of other professors who had lectured internationally, the focus of Dr. Hoffman's teaching was not to ensure that Western psychological theories were "correctly" applied to other cultures but instead to look for ways in which Western psychology could complement or learn from other cultural perspectives. This was the first time in all my years of formal education that I was invited to intentionally focus on integrating indigenous cultural wisdom rather than imposing existing values upon an Indigenous population. This invitation offered the opportunity to bring all of me into the space without needing to split my identity or translate my way of being in the world or prioritize the status quo and colonial mindset as the de facto "correct" way to be.

As a founding member of the Task Force on Indigenous Psychology, Dr. Hoffman asserts that the aims of indigenous psychology are to examine the colonization and hegemony of Western psychology while strengthening the voices of Indigenous practitioners. I would add here that part of the colonization of psychology is the cultural appropriation of practices that are brought into Western psychology and adapted to fit a Western audience. Much like Yoga being practiced without acknowledging its spiritual foundations, concepts such as mindfulness and Zen have been bastardized for a Western palate. Bringing attention to these types of processes is important for cultivating true inclusion in any profession.

We don't know what we don't know, and when our eyes are opened it can be a humbling experience. It can be disconcerting, uncomfortable, and we might dip into feelings of shame. As someone who professes to be attuned to issues of diversity and inclusion, it blew my mind that I

---

[2] Indigenous psychology refers to the study of psychological phenomena in the cultural and historical context of the population, as opposed to working with imported theories from an external culture.

hadn't questioned some of the origins of the theories I had swallowed whole throughout my therapy training. Unearthing my own internalized racism toward Chinese culture and values was also disorienting, but it was absolutely essential to my development as a practitioner. Getting clear about not only what my values are but also where they come from was hugely liberating.

Students and graduates of The HERD Institute® will be familiar with me talking about the importance of being able to sit in discomfort and breathe through to possibilities. In the current political climate, I'm struck by how evident it is, now more than ever before, that we need to sit in discomfort when we are faced with difference—difference in modalities, difference in philosophy, difference in beliefs, and difference in cultures. One of my mentors, Dr. Kirk Schneider, co-founder of the Existential–Humanistic Institute in California, recently released a book called *The Depolarizing of America: A Guidebook for Social Healing*.[3] In it, Dr. Schneider suggests that polarization is steeped in fear and discomfort which prevents us from being able to be open to dialogue. The "antidote" is the cultivation of a sense of awe, which he defines as a sense of humility or wonder, or a sense of adventure towards living. In cultivating our capacity for awe, we can step into a place of curiosity rather than judgments, and in so doing, promote true dialogue.

True dialogue necessitates the willingness to experience the other's perspective, however uncomfortable, and to allow that experience to change us. True dialogue is not necessarily one without disagreements. When we speak authentically, there is always a risk for vulnerability and discomfort. True dialogue prioritizes getting *real* over being palatable.

The danger of wanting conversations about social justice to be nice and comfortable is that it can perpetuate the status quo. Best-selling author Austin Channing Brown says that, "When you believe niceness disproves the presence of racism, it's easy to start believing bigotry is rare...it obligates me to be nice in return, rather than truthful."[4] And while I understand how vulnerable it feels to not know what to say in case I say it wrong, and how misunderstood I feel when my good intentions are called out when they don't translate in terms of the

---

[3] Schneider, K. J. (2020). *The depolarizing of America: A guidebook for social healing*. University Professors Press.

[4] Channing Brown, A. (2018). *I'm still here: Black dignity in a world made for whiteness*. Convergent Books, p. 101.

impact I had intended, I also know that the moment I am pulled to respond defensively, I have already lost my ability to listen and be open for dialogue.

I am writing this in the aftermath of the mass shooting in Uvalde, Texas, where an 18-year-old gunman opened fire at an elementary school. Nineteen students and two teachers were killed, and seventeen other people were wounded. In the days following the massacre, much like in the aftermath of George Floyd's murder in 2020, organizations around the country released positional statements about the incident. I posted a statement on social media and sent it out as a newsletter to our network of contacts. Like others, I felt compelled to say *something* in response to this horrific act, to take a clear stand that the normalizing of mass shootings was not acceptable, and to offer support to members of our community by acknowledging this. I felt firm in my conviction that this statement would be received as intended and, as always, my writing-as-activism process helped to soothe my own heartache.

"I was trying to figure out how to address this so I'm just gonna come out and ask...Texas got a newsletter but Buffalo didn't?" It was a simple text from my dear friend and HERD faculty member, Elizabeth McCorvey.

Ouf.

Ouch.

I noticed the edges of shame that crept up within me. To clarify, Elizabeth's text was referring to the mass shooting at a supermarket in Buffalo, a week prior to Uvalde, where ten Black people were killed, and three others were injured. The reaction from the general public, the news cycle, and social media to the Buffalo shooting had been a momentary sharp intake of breath, thoughts, and prayers, and a feeling of resignation. There were certainly no uproar, indignation, or position statements in the way that the Uvalde shooting had elicited.

I had worked hard to craft my statement about Uvalde, and in response to my creeping shame, I could feel the indignation in defense of being criticized. I took a breath to allow myself a moment's pause. My friend was hurting from yet another example that confirmed for her that Black bodies are not prioritized. I knew that it wasn't that she didn't feel the horror of Uvalde, and I knew that she wasn't attacking me. It wouldn't have been helpful to either of us at that moment for me to express my shame or guilt to her. I didn't want her to feel like she needed to offer me platitudes for my misstep. I certainly didn't want her to feel that my shame was her responsibility, or that I wasn't robust enough in my ability to hear her challenge and still hold space for our relationship. Regardless of my intention, I had created a rupture in our relationship that I needed to take accountability for.

"Thank you for naming that. Not going to make excuses for not addressing both. I see how my statement is incomplete. I'm sorry for causing you more hurt and appreciate you challenging me with it. I know you didn't need to expend that emotional labor but I'm glad you're willing to go there with me."

Through this exchange, we were able to have a deeper conversation about what this moment meant for us, our friendship, and how we can trust each other to hold a sense of relational safety when difficulties arise. In prioritizing our relationship over our discomfort, we were able to step into true dialogue. What may have resulted in an irreparable rupture turned into a precious moment of connection. I am thankful for Elizabeth's courage in challenging me, reminding me that despite being a person of color, despite experiencing and understanding what it means to belong to a marginalized group myself, I am not exempt from the need to continue to educate myself about the experiences of others in marginalized groups. Ultimately, I am also a product of the system that I exist within.

Reflection Questions

When was the last time you felt defensive in a conversation? What would have helped in that moment? What was important to you? What conversations have you had lately that you would like to rewind and redo?

Part II

Braver Conversations

Chapter 9

Learning to be BRAVER

Assumptions

I'm going to make some assumptions about you, the reader, that feels important to name. I'm going to assume that you have chosen to read this book in order to deepen your understanding of what it means to work within a culturally competent framework, and know that this is an ongoing endeavor in cultural humility. I'm going to assume that reading this book means you understand that cultural competencies are built over time and not achieved as an end goal in one sitting. I'm going to assume that you have some connections to the equine industry in general and/or with equine-facilitated work. I'm also going to assume that for some of you, I might be preaching to the choir. More important, I'm going to assume that for some of you, there will be a healthy dose of skepticism, and I expect that your worldview is going to be vastly different from mine. And that's okay.

I'm also going to assume that by getting to Part 2 of this book, you may have experienced some strong emotions, grappled with some concepts, and perhaps even thrown this book across the room in indignation, frustration, or anger but have come out the other side still willing to engage and learn. I want you to know that I appreciate your commitment, resilience, and courage.

As a transplant to the United States, I feel like I've been on a steep learning curve in my attempt to understand the deep socioeconomic–political–racial divides that exist here that are unique to this country but also familiar and translatable to systems of inequality around the world. In recent conversations with HERD Institute community members, I have shared some of my experiences of being culturally different in the US compared to the UK. For me, it's much easier to grasp the complexities of these concepts when presented with real life examples. In the following chapters, we'll begin to unpack some of the terminology used in conversations about social justice through a collection of reflective pieces and anecdotes of real-life encounters.

Relational Engagement

My colleagues and I encourage our students to pay attention to what is happening in the here and now. We focus on the awareness of self, other, and environment. What is happening for me? What is happening between us? What is happening around us? Eugene Gendlin, author of *Focusing,* says, "Moment by moment, after anything either person says or does, one must attend to the effect it has on what is directly experienced."[1]

Research indicates that developing critical consciousness (the ability to recognize and analyze systems of inequality and commitment to take action), a term coined by Brazilian educator Paulo Freire, not only broadens the perspective of students and increases academic achievement and engagement but also increases their commitment to challenging systemic injustice.[2] This sense of community activism fosters a sense of engagement and connection and alleviates feelings of isolation and powerlessness that are prevalent among marginalized populations. Critical consciousness also necessitates the cultivation of what Isobel Wilkerson, author of *Caste: The Origins of Our Discontent,* calls radical empathy.

> Radical empathy means putting in the work to educate oneself and to listen with a humble heart to understand another's experience from their perspective, not as we imagine we would feel. Radical empathy is not about you and what you think you would do in a situation you have never been in and perhaps never will. It is the kindred connection from a place of deep knowing that opens your spirit to the pain of another as they perceive it.[3]

That's a tough ask. It sounds great in theory, but how does that work in practice? It can only happen when we place the relationship at the center of the interaction. In their book *Teaching Diversity Relationally: Engaging emotions and embracing possibilities,* psychology professors Kim, Donovan, and Suyemoto suggest that students become more engaged in diversity classes when they are taught from an emotional

---

[1] Gendlin E. T. (1981). *Focusing* (2nd ed.). Bantam Books.
[2] Freire P. (2005). *Education for critical consciousness.* Continuum.
[3] Wilkerson I. (2020). *Caste: The origins of our discontents.* Random House.

and relational framework.[4] They offer five foundational elements for engagement:

1) Cultivating reflexivity and exploration of positionality
2) Engaging emotions
3) Encouraging agency and responsibility
4) Fostering perspective taking
5) Promoting community and relational learning

These five elements align with the HERD approach of raising awareness of self, other, and environment. By encouraging students to reflect on what is happening for them and exploring the context of the student's perspective (i.e., positionality), they can begin to access what is happening internally, move toward naming the emotions that arise, and take accountability for their own responses. This focus on the intrapersonal (awareness of self) helps to provide some grounding prior to engaging with others. By fostering and practicing the art of seeing a situation from another's perspective, we can start to bring awareness to what is happening *between* individuals and acknowledge the impact on the relationship (awareness of other). By promoting community and relational learning, we can look at the bigger picture (awareness of environment) and the holistic impact of responses.

Overlaying these elements, Kim and her colleagues also identify four intentional practices that enhance learning: curiosity about the other's experience; humility to accept that we don't know what we don't know; self-compassion for mistakes we make; and mindfulness of each moment. Embracing these practices opens the door toward prioritizing the relationships within these conversations over the temptation to stay entrenched within our own perspective.

How to be BRAVER

I appreciate these four intentional *practices.* I emphasize practice because I recognize that these are active, rather than passive, processes. To stay curious, we have to ask questions, which leads us to a humbling experience of challenging how we know what we know, and why we believe what we believe. As you read the following chapters, you'll be given prompts to pause and reflect on what you've read. Take

---

[4] Kim, G. S., Donovan, R. A., & Suyemoto, K. L. (2022). *Teaching diversity relationally: Engaging emotions and embracing possibilities.* Routledge.

this opportunity to notice what you are feeling. The more we increase our awareness of what is happening in each moment, the more choices we have in how we respond, intrapersonally and interpersonally. We have to actively find self-compassion and be mindful of how to accept what we were previously unaware of, or for missteps we take. But as Maya Angelou so elegantly said, "Do the best you can until you know better. Then when you know better, do better."[5]

My intention for this book is for us to have braver conversations that support our ability to create more intentionally inclusive spaces. This, in turn, will help us to access our embodied experiences so that we can cultivate an embodied sense of belonging for ourselves and others.

I want to offer a pathway for these conversations by engaging in an active process of being BRAVER. You've already had a sneak peek at some of this in the format of the reflection questions in Part 1:

> Breathe
> Reflect
> Accept
> Vulnerable
> Engage
> Reflect

I invite you to practice this as you read the following chapters and/or the next time you are part of a conversation about diversity, equity, and inclusion. Remember, this is an *active practice*. The more you practice, the more it will become a way of being rather than something you "do."

Breathe: Notice your breath. Pay attention to when you're holding your breath. Pay attention to when your breath becomes shallower. In those moments when you come across a word or phrase that brings up an emotional response, take a moment to focus on your breath. Name the emotions one by one. Notice what happens in your body. Allow yourself to conduct a full-body scan and notice where there might be tension. There's no need to "do" anything immediately with whatever is coming up for you; simply notice and breathe.

Reflect: Allow yourself to be curious about what came up for you. What surprised you and/or what did you learn about yourself in that moment? What do you want to know more about? What might you be fearful of? What might you be protective of? If you're in a brave conversation, what is the nature of your relationships among those you

---

[5] Retrieved from https://www.goodreads.com/author/quotes/3503.Maya_Angelou

are engaging with? What do you want to honor in these relationships? What might you be prioritizing in this moment over the relationships?

Accept: This is an exercise in radical acceptance of whatever is showing up authentically. Activate your self-compassion toward whatever emotions are present. This is a non-judgmental process of discovering how you are responding in the moment. Know that these feelings are valid and part of your journey of self-discovery. Accept that this is hard and complex and that you may never fully understand the other's perspective. Accept that despite your willingness and intention, you still might make mistakes. Accept your part in how the conversation is going.

Vulnerable: What might feel risky and vulnerable at this moment? Ask yourself, what is it that makes this feel vulnerable? If you're in the midst of a brave conversation, what might make you feel more vulnerable? Ask yourself, what risks are you willing to take to deepen the relationship in this moment, if at all? If you don't feel safe to lean into that risk, then what are your choices? What might it feel like to name your vulnerability, to share that in your conversation? What do you need right now from this interaction?

Engage: What would be the optimal outcome of this conversation? To feel heard? To feel validated? To feel seen? To be right? To connect and deepen the relationship with the person/people you are in conversation with? To hold your boundaries and be okay with not changing the other's mind? Being clear about what we want from this moment helps us to know how to engage in the conversation moving forward.

Reflect: Always, always take time to reflect on what you experienced as a result of engaging in the conversation. What might you do or say differently—right now and/or the next time you speak? Does the conversation feel complete at this moment? If not, is there space/time/energy for more? What surprised you about this interaction? What did you learn from the experience? How have you been changed or impacted by this?

As we learn these steps to be BRAVER, we can translate this way of being into all areas of our lives, in all interactions, in all relationships. In stepping into relationships with a BRAVER framework, I've noticed that I am much more able to regulate my responses to conversations that have previously sent me into emotional turmoil and have deepened my relationships to those around me with whom I am being braver. This process has also supported me in my relationships with my equine partners and other non-human animal relationships in my life. I'm much more able to pause and reflect on what might be happening *for them*, rather than impose my instinctive, habitual interpretation or perspective. I find myself adopting less anthropomorphic and human-centric ways of communicating with my non-human animal companions, which inevitably has led me down many rabbit holes of additional theories and perspectives to ponder (more on that later). For me, the aim in all of these interactions with humans or non-human animals is to deepen our understanding of the other and to find a sense of belonging to/with our self, other, and the environment.

In the following chapters, I invite you to practice the art of being BRAVER as you walk with me through a few stories. If you are reading this book on your own, it may be helpful to journal your reflections as you practice being BRAVER. If you're reading this as part of a book club, class, or workshop, you may want to take each chapter at a time and attend to this process individually, and then share your reflections with one another. The invitation to practice this process extends to those of you who are already familiar with social justice work as well as those of you who are just beginning your journey in learning about issues of diversity, equity, and inclusion. Perhaps you'll recognize yourself in these experiences. Perhaps you'll feel called to action in some way. Perhaps you'll feel angry or frustrated. And if you feel discomfort, take a breath and sit with it, and breathe through to possibilities. Let's practice being braver together.

Chapter 10

What My Chickens Are Teaching Me About Diversity & Inclusion

Yes, you read that right. I'm talking about my chickens.

I've had a backyard flock of chickens now for the last seven years. Learning to raise chickens has been an eye-opening process full of joy and heartbreak. Those of you who have been to The HERD Institute® headquarters will know how much my colleague Sarah Morehouse and I love our "chick chicks." In the beginning, I chose to start my flock with six beautiful feathered friends named Zelda, Griffin, Buffy, Ophelia, Daphne, and Buckbeak. These girls would free range our farm in Ohio during the day. They hid in the bushes, climbed the manure pile, nested in the stalls, and joined in with client sessions and teaching workshops. They brought hilarity in moments that needed levity and insight during profound times of learning. They demonstrated the indisputable fact of their sentient nature through their unique personalities.

Over the years, we've lost our girls to sickness and predators and, of the original six, only Zelda and Griffin remain. We've added to the flock and now have a couple of three-year-olds (Henrietta and Martha) and a couple of younger ones around two years old (Libby and Bessie). We also fostered a couple of adult chickens (Blanche and Dorothy) for a couple of months in the summer of 2020 before rehoming them. Each time we begin to integrate the flock with new arrivals, I am fascinated by how they build relationships with one another.

Much like horses, dogs, and other animals, chickens have been perceived as having distinct social structures based on the dominance theory of "pecking order," where individuals within a group have a social standing that is reserved for the one who exhibits the most dominant behavior. While this dominance theory has been challenged in relation to horses and dogs, it is still regarded as fact for chickens. What I've observed in my own flock is that this theory only holds true if we equate dominance with aggression and power. This comes to light most often when new birds are being introduced to the flock. My established flock of four (Zelda, Griffin, Martha, and Henrietta) are a fairly egalitarian group. Griffin is the matriarch that the others turn to when there is a threat. Zelda is the most likely to guard resources and chase others away from food. Martha pushes boundaries by regularly escaping the chicken run but has no sense of personal space and will regularly bump into or jump on the others when she gets excited. Henrietta is the broodiest and will claim her space at the nesting box and push others out of her way if needed. To focus on dominance only in terms of power and status would miss the nuanced interactions that form the fabric of the social structure within the flock.

When we fostered Blanche and Dorothy, I quickly recognized that they were not going to mix well with the rest of the flock. Blanche was physically much bigger and stronger than all the others and introduced herself by way of stretching her neck upwards and puffing herself up to her fullest extent. She charged at the others, randomly striking and pecking at them as she went. She flapped her wings and landed on top of Martha, who valiantly fought back and wrestled free. Dorothy then followed Blanche on her rampage by pinning Henrietta to the ground. I stepped in and separated them.

Traditional backyard chicken owners recommend introducing new birds to the flock over a period of time, extending the time of contact with each session until they are comfortable with one another and have established their pecking order. It's a given that there will be some scuffles before things work themselves out. I had used this method of introduction with Henrietta and Martha the year before, and while there were a few minor pecks and a bit of jostling, there was never any targeted aggression like I was seeing with Blanche and Dorothy. After a couple more attempts at integrating them that led to similar results, I decided to keep them separated for the duration of their stay while I looked to rehome them. Thankfully, my neighbors decided that they wanted to start keeping chickens, and I was able to rehome them with ease. They now have free range access to forage under shrubs and bushes and follow my neighbors to their patio for treats. There are no other chickens, so their aggressive behaviors have disappeared.

I could have let nature take its course and allowed the flock to "self-regulate" and find its own equilibrium, ignoring the stress signals that the girls were demonstrating, believing that they'd get over it. I could have subscribed to the idea that a pecking order was necessary and the Darwinian notion of survival of the fittest would balance things out. I could have told myself that they're only chickens and maybe I was anthropormophizing the whole thing and it was really not as bad as it seemed.

What I knew for sure was this: for the entire time that Blanche and Dorothy were in residence with us, overall egg production went down by 50%. As soon as I rehomed them, egg production went back to normal. The girls were also more willing to engage with me and much less anxious about going into the chicken run during the day.

This process got me thinking about racial and social justice work and what it means to be an activist. It brought to light the difference between attending to the *symptoms* of systemic issues rather than actively dismantling the power structures that perpetuate them. Stepping in to break up a fight between the chickens would be an intervention that addressed the symptoms of the system. Removing Blanche and Dorothy and rehabilitating them in an environment where they didn't need to exhibit those aggressive behaviors dismantled the system. It's worth noting that I took Blanche and Dorothy in because their previous owner was sick and could no longer care for them. They had been living in a relatively small coop with no space to free range and had to fight for resources with others. It's not that they were inherently "bad chickens," simply that they had learned they had to fight to survive.

Clearly, dismantling systems of power is not so easy in human terms. But we can think about which leaders we might want to remove from power, and what resources we have, both individually and collectively, that can help us to do that. We can work to unpick the fabric we have woven that supports the dominance, oppression, and supremacy over others and look for ways to empower, support, and celebrate them instead.

As I integrated my youngest chickens, Libby and Bessie, into the flock, I hoped for a smooth transition while welcoming the increased diversity that they bring to the flock (if we ever meet in person, I can tell you all about their different breeds and how I can tell which chick has laid which egg!). I trusted that my matriarch, Griffin, would take them under her wing and help to build their confidence. Most of all, I hoped that the newcomers would feel a sense of safety and belonging and make themselves a home.

Practice Being BRAVER

Breathe. Notice what is happening in your bodily being.
Reflect. What do you resonate with? Notice your bodily response to the words dominance, power, and dismantling systems. What does dominance mean for you? What does power mean? What is your understanding of your role in this context? Has this story challenged any assumptions or beliefs you hold?
Accept what is emerging in the moment. All of it. Whatever you are feeling, allow it to surface and name your emotions.
Vulnerable. What feels vulnerable right now? What feels risky?
Engage with this story. How do you want to respond? What do you want to say?
Reflect. What are you taking away from this experience?

Chapter 11

Am I Safe?

At the beginning of 2020, the COVID-19 virus had only just started to seep into the consciousness of some people in the United States. My parents live in Hong Kong, so I had been aware of the virus spreading in China since November 2019. By the end of January, the momentum of the news cycle had picked up, and the virus had begun its journey around the globe. Soon after, I became wary of what felt like a shift of other's perception of me as an Asian woman as I went out and about in my daily life. Were people giving me a wide berth? Were people looking at me suspiciously? Maybe it was all in my head and I had nothing to fear.

Flying back to Florida from California at the beginning of February, I was faced with some blatant racism. The woman who was supposed to be sitting in the middle seat next to me asked to be moved as she was "concerned about sitting next to an Asian person." She was upgraded. I soothed myself from my quiet outrage by stretching out into her empty seat.

Toward the end of February, I went to our local Chinese restaurant. It was eerily quiet on a Friday night as people had started to avoid Chinese food from fear of contracting the virus. Same thing at our local Asian market. The owner told me that business was down because non-Asian folks were too scared to go in. These experiences, combined with news reports of the increase in racial assaults on Asian people around the country, meant that I could no longer gaslight myself. My fears were real.

I found solace during the lockdown. I was privileged to have been able to take refuge on our farm, secluded and stocked with enough provisions to wait it out. I felt thankful that I could retreat from my own fear of being a target for others' fear-induced prejudice. By isolating myself on the farm, I didn't have to worry about being spit on by strangers or endure suspicion of being contagious due to the color of my skin, or risk being subjected to verbal attacks to go back to my own country, either thrown in my face or muttered in passing.

As the world began to lift pandemic restrictions, I started to wonder what being Asian in a post-pandemic world might look like. I knew that I had many safe spaces to retreat to: my farm, my friends and colleagues, and our HERD community. I knew that I wasn't alone in my fears. Existentially, this anxiety stemmed from asking the question, "Am I safe?" And when I asked that question, I recognized that it applied to so many layers of our society.

In terms of Maslow's hierarchy of needs, we have all experienced on some level a challenge to our pre-pandemic sense of safety. Am I physically safe? From others? For others? Because ultimately, it is not only about whether I feel safe personally, but how we can create safety for everyone. As I pondered what the impact of the pandemic might be, back in those early days of naively thinking that it would be over by the summer of 2020, I wrote the following in my journal:

> *"Perhaps this pandemic can be a wake-up call for those who have never previously needed to be attuned to feelings of safety, of being on alert, or constantly seeking a safe space. Perhaps it will help those of us in our privileged lives to have more compassion for those who seek help and refuge, give us a clearer understanding of what it might be like to have post-traumatic stress responses, and provide a foundation for cultivating empathy. I hope that's the case. I hope that we can re-emerge from this collective trauma with resilience. I hope that we'll be safe."*

Practice Being BRAVER

Breathe and notice what's coming up for you. **Reflect** on what this brought up for you about the early days of the pandemic. What were you most concerned about? What felt safe or dangerous to you then? What about now? What are you aware of in hearing about my fears? **Accept** whatever is emerging. What feels **vulnerable** for you right now? What might feel risky to name? **Engage** with this story. How might you have responded as a witness to the incident on the flight? **Reflect.** What are you taking away from this experience?

Chapter 12

NIMBY Attitudes

There had been distinct grumblings in the midwestern suburban bubble that I lived in. A new family had just moved in a few doors down from a friend of mine, and as customary in the land of the white picket fences, the neighbors were out in force to get a glimpse of the newcomers. It transpired that the new arrivals were a white single mom with three Black kids: two elementary school-aged daughters and a 20-year-old son. The neighborhood watchers reported that the son did not seem to be in college or otherwise gainfully employed. Instead, he spent most of his time in his garage tinkering with his car but never driving it anywhere. As the stories trickled through the grapevine, it became clear to me that the son had learning disabilities and was most likely autistic. His eccentric behavior, lack of social skills, and obsession with his car had already earned him the label of 'the weird guy' on the street.

On a night out with several women from the neighborhood, the topic of the new residents came up. One woman was particularly upset by this young man's behavior and alarmed at what dangers he might pose to her children. When I pointed out that it sounded like he had special needs, it was taken as evidence that he was a threat to society and the conversation turned toward school shootings and the number of cases where people with special needs and/or mental health problems had committed horrific crimes "in the ghettos." The tirade ended with her stating that she would rather not have these types of people living next door.

> **Practice Being BRAVER**
>
> **Breathe.** What do you notice? **Reflect** on this scenario and identify what assumptions you may have made. **Accept** what is coming up for you. What feels **vulnerable** right now? **Engage** with the story. How might you respond to this tirade? **Reflect.** What did you learn about yourself through your response?

Continuing the Story...

I was the only person of color in the group. As I looked around the table, I saw a few people nodding their heads in agreement, and I realized that I was faced with an all too familiar choice: to engage in the dismantling of unconscious biases or smile and nod and be complicit in my silence. Internally, I was raging against the undercurrents of racism that I was witnessing. It would have been easy for me to counter this tirade with an angry, frustrated, and indignant response. I could have argued against the dominant, white, middle-class, and insular perspective that this woman represented in the hope of opening her eyes to a more diverse world. I could have made judgments about her and ridiculed the values that she holds dear in an effort to get my point across.

I didn't respond in that vein then, and I most likely won't when this kind of thing happens again. I'm aware of how much energy the process of swallowing my anger takes. I'm also aware that I have to choose my battles.

Her "Not In My Backyard" (NIMBY) attitude is shared by many people in the area. It is partly why suburbs exist. It speaks to the perpetuation of segregation between the haves and have-nots across racial divides and the pretense that if the issues aren't visible, they don't exist. Prior experiences of similar exchanges had taught me that responding in a judgmental, angry, and indignant way will merely fuel this separation. So, while my instinct was to rage, I found myself searching hard for some compassion in order to engage in a conversation that didn't involve a right or wrong response to the issue. Instead, I told her that while I heard that she felt fearful, I also had a different perspective. I told her about my work as a therapeutic riding instructor and the families with special needs kids that I serve. I told her that I can only imagine how difficult life must be for a single parent juggling work, family, and therapies for their grown son. I wondered aloud about whether this family is new to the area and whether they are aware of what assistance might be available. I told her of the bullying that autistic children are often subjected to. The conversation soon turned to a discussion on the importance of teaching children to be more tolerant of difference.

Practice Being BRAVER

Breathe. Notice what is happening for you. In this reflection, are you able to identify the BRAVER steps in the scenario? What was risky? What was vulnerable in the moment? What are you feeling now? What might you have done/said differently? What are you taking away from this experience?

Side Note: The Aim is Not to Avoid Conflict

As an existential therapist, I value the importance of empathy and compassion as a way of relating. Differences of opinion can provide depth to our encounters with another. Indeed, it is often through the discovery of these differences that we truly begin to see the other. NIMBY attitudes not only stem from a lack of compassion but also from a lack of awareness. Modeling compassion opens the door for others to feed into their own capacity for it and increases awareness of issues that might otherwise be ignored. Compassion allows us to present a different opinion without the drive to annihilate and/or shame the other. It allows me to take a breath and say, "I can understand why you might say that. I believe in something different," offering a new perspective without the conversation escalating into conflict.

This is not to say that conflict needs to be avoided at all cost. I am not saying that there is no place for anger and indignation when faced with discrimination, only that in this context I recognized that by attacking her values I would have contributed to her evidence for the need to distance herself from the important discussions on diversity. Given that I chose to live in this neighborhood, I also needed to take some responsibility for what happens in it. I know that different responses will elicit different results depending on the context of these conversations. In this instance, through modeling a compassionate approach I was able to campaign peacefully against the NIMBY mentality and bring a little more tolerance for diversity into my backyard.

Being BRAVER

Notice what your reactions are to this anecdote. Pay attention to your breath. What are you feeling? What resonates with you from this description? Whose perspective are you drawn to more? Whose perspective are you more familiar with? Were there specific words that caught your attention or triggered a specific response?

Chapter 13

Recognizing White Privilege, Owning Our Biases, and Accepting Different Perspectives

I noticed that even now, as I recalled the experience in the last chapter, my breath became shallower and I clenched my jaw, so I consciously took a deep breath and focused on releasing my facial muscles. At the time, I remember feeling similar sensations in my body and holding my breath. I remember wondering if this woman's reactions would have been the same had this been a white family and a young white man. I wondered if she would have felt less fearful if that had been the case. I felt a familiar tug of anger about living in a society that has such a deeply embedded fear of Black men, and while I acknowledge that this isn't directly her fault, I felt angry at my neighbor for perpetuating this injustice. From my perspective, there were clear undercurrents of white privilege throughout the conversation and more than a sprinkling of overt prejudice toward those who do not fit into the homogeneous environment we were in.

The term white privilege elicits strong reactions from many people and inspires dismissal from those who do not feel that they have been afforded advantages in life. So, let's be clear. When I use the term white privilege, it doesn't mean that I am assuming that life has been easy and without struggle, or that your accomplishments are unearned. It means that the color of your skin is not something that has been part of your struggle and that your skin color is the default setting in the world around you. It means that as a child, you never had to wonder what Crayola to use when coloring in people; it means that you are able to see yourself represented in the world around you; it means you can succeed without being told that you're a credit to your people; and it means a whole host of things that are mostly invisible to you but are daily struggles for people of color. Peggy McIntosh, an anti-racism researcher and activist, published an article in 1988 entitled "White

Privilege: Unpacking the Invisible Knapsack" that lists many more examples of the advantages of existing in a white body.[1]

White privilege also means that you can be involved in conversations like the one described in the previous chapter, when someone refers to "the ghetto" and "these types of people," without wondering if you are also under suspicion. The undertones of racial prejudice were inherent in her assumption that Black men will bring crime and lower the tone in the neighborhood.

Being BRAVER

Breathe: Notice what's happening in your body. **Reflect:** As you read the story, were you aware of leaning into that stereotype? Were you empathizing with her fear? Perhaps you agreed with her? Or did you notice something different? A sense of injustice and a call to action? A feeling of indignation at her ignorance? Or did you respond in your body with a resigned sigh of familiarity? **Accept:** Whatever you feel is okay, because this is part of our journey in becoming more culturally competent. Awareness without judgment, or the process of bringing into consciousness what we were blind to previously, is key. Your reactions are the result of a lifetime's worth of cultural messaging that we unconsciously rely on, like the air around us and like water to a fish. **Vulnerable:** What feels risky to you now? What would have felt risky if you had been part of this conversation? **Engage:** What do you need to express now? What do you need in this moment? **Reflect:** What did you learn from this experience?

In the process of examining our own biases, we may be surprised at our reactions. In talking about this experience later with a close friend who had witnessed this exchange, she admitted that she didn't hear undertones of racism in the conversation. She was, however, aware that our mutual acquaintance was perhaps more agitated than she needed to be, and that she didn't feel that the young man was a threat. Instead, she was curious as to why we hadn't invited the new neighbor to our

---

[1] McIntosh, P. (2003). White privilege: Unpacking the invisible knapsack. In S. Plous (Ed.), *Understanding prejudice and discrimination* (pp. 191–196). McGraw-Hill.

gathering and had planned on going over to introduce herself the next day. She was appreciative of what I had highlighted about the new neighbor possibly needing support. I appreciated her willingness to share her perspective with me. It also reminded me to move away from a polarized stance. My friend's spirit of abundance allowed me to see that I was also making assumptions about this family. Her approach was to go to the source to get to know them.

Chapter 14

White Faces in White Spaces

Who Are You Serving?

Within the equine-facilitated world, we pride ourselves on the diversity of programs that we offer to our communities. In terms of age, gender, physical and cognitive abilities, emotional and mental health challenges, occupations, and trauma survivors, an extensive range of services meets the needs of those most vulnerable in our communities. Research has been conducted within the field for programs serving veterans, first responders, survivors of human trafficking, marginalized youth, cancer patients, dementia and Alzheimer's patients, neurodivergent populations, and those suffering from depression, anxiety, eating disorders, post-traumatic stress, traumatic brain injuries, as well as those dealing with physical disabilities. There is an ongoing need for further research to establish more evidence-based frameworks in our field, but we are all working toward contributing to the wider field in incredible ways.

What's startling to me in looking at the topics being researched within the field are the missing populations: Black, Indigenous, and people of color, and folks who identify as part of the LGBTQIA community. The Agency for Healthcare Research and Quality (AHRQ) defines health disparities as

> differences in access to or availability of medical facilities and services and variation in rates of disease occurrence and disabilities between population groups defined by socioeconomic characteristics such as age, ethnicity, economic resources, or gender and populations identified geographically.[1]

---

[1] AHRQ (n.d) Disparities. Retrieved from https://www.ahrq.gov/topics/disparities. html#:~:text=Healthcare%20disparities%20are%20differences%20in,or%20gender %20and%20populations%20identified

Health disparities related to race, ethnicity, and socioeconomic status indicate that Black, Indigenous, and people of color are more likely to suffer from higher rates of heart disease, obesity, diabetes, cancer, and other chronic conditions that lead to premature death. These disparities exist due to factors such as poverty, lack of nutritious food, lack of access to medical care and/or insurance, and lack of adequate support systems. Health disparities became increasingly evident at the beginning of the global pandemic when Black, Indigenous, and people of color in the United States experienced higher rates of Covid-19 related hospitalization and death compared to white populations. This was partly due to these populations occupying a majority of frontline positions within healthcare, retail, and other essential services, and partly due to the pre-existing inequities within public health systems. For LGBTQIA communities, research conducted by The Trevor Project in 2022 indicates that 45% of LGBTQIA youth had seriously considered suicide in the past year, and 73% reported symptoms of anxiety and depression.[2] These are sobering statistics that speak to the need for these kids to feel validated in their right to exist, to be seen and heard, and the importance of creating spaces to experience a sense of belonging to the world.

Bringing these disparities into the context of the equine-facilitated field, if we are working with marginalized populations, we need to be aware of the challenges that our service users face. The ambiguous label of "at-risk youth" is used to encapsulate a host of issues that these youths are more likely to experience, including failure to graduate from high school, domestic violence, sexual abuse, teen pregnancy, drug and alcohol addiction, homelessness, health disparities, and death by suicide, to name a few. While Black, Indigenous and youth of color and LGBTQIA youth constitute a majority of those who are deemed at risk, there is scant literature and research to address these disparities within equine-facilitated programs. There is also a lack of quantitative data on the disparities within the client populations that our equine-facilitated programs serve.

Meanwhile, according to a recent survey of PATH International members, the demographics of service providers are predominantly white, middle-class, middle-aged women. While data are not available for sexual orientation, my lived experience within the organization and

---

[2] National survey on LGBTQ youth mental health, 2022. The Trevor Project. Retrieved from https://www.thetrevorproject.org/survey-2022/

the equine-facilitated field in general would lead me to guess that the majority of providers are also cisgender and heterosexual. In short, there is a startling lack of diversity within the industry at large. We exist in a very white and heteronormative space.

Black Lives Matter (Too) in White Spaces

We cannot talk about white privilege without also talking about white spaces. And we cannot talk about white privilege and white spaces without mentioning the phrase "Black Lives Matter," particularly in the United States. I'll go further to say that if you are working with Black youth in your programs and you are still responding to the phrase "Black Lives Matter" with "All lives matter," you need to go home. Go home and do your homework. Go home and educate yourself. Because if you enter a space where power dynamics are already inherently skewed toward the dominant culture, where you are in the position to influence young minds, and you don't understand why this response is problematic, you do not have the cultural competence to teach or lead black youth. Period.

Here's why: White privilege exists because of generations of public and social policies that deliberately prevented Black, Indigenous, and people of color from participating in society on an equal footing to people of European descent. In the United States, the Civil Rights Act was passed into law in 1964, and while there is more openness now for integration, there are still pockets of resistance fueled by fear of infringement on white rights and assumed privileges. And while it's more comfortable to think that the term "racist" only applies to people who openly and actively voice white supremacy rhetoric, it would be naïve of us to think that these attitudes have not become internalized in more subtle ways. Almost six decades later, we can see how white privilege sought to maintain and protect white spaces by the fact that there are still overwhelmingly white neighborhoods, schools, organizations, sports, and places of worship. Elijah Anderson, Professor of Sociology and African American Studies at Yale University, comments that these white spaces are seen as "unremarkable, or as normal, taken-for-granted reflections" of society by white folks. Fish don't know what water is. In contrast, Black, Indigenous, and people of color will enter these spaces with care and "reflexively note the proportion of whites to

Blacks...when judging a setting as too white, they can feel uneasy and consider it to be informally off limits."[3]

I dated a white guy in college who came from a working-class town on the outskirts of Birmingham, England. Generations of his family had worked in the car assembly plant in town, and he was the first person in his family to go to college. While the metropolitan area of Birmingham was relatively diverse, the town he grew up in was not. For a while, he took pride in introducing me to the rural village pubs that he and his friends and family regularly frequented. He was oblivious to the hushed silence that would descend momentarily as we entered these premises and unaware of the stares that followed me around the room. I was distinctly on edge and uncomfortable. Initially, when I told him how I felt, he dismissed me by saying he hadn't noticed anything of the sort, and I must be imagining it. It wasn't until I asked him to pay attention the next time it happened that he admitted that it wasn't something that he'd ever needed to consider. For me, that's the crux of the privilege of white spaces: If you don't need to think about it, then it's a privilege.

Which leads us back to the phrase, "Black Lives Matter." Drs. Louis Hoffman, Nathaniel Granger Jr., and Lisa Vallejos, leading authors on multiculturalism and diversity and existential psychology, stated the following:

> saying "Black Lives Matter" never intended to suggest that other lives do not matter. Rather, the implicit message in stating, "Black Lives Matter" is "All lives matter, but our society acts as if Black lives do not matter; therefore, we need to be explicit that Black lives also matter in order for all lives to matter." ...Black Lives Matter is not antipolice, antigovernment, or anti-White people, and it is not a group that promotes or intends to incite violence of any kind. While some individuals who may use the phrase "Black Lives Matter" have been violent, this should not be confused with the intentions of the movement any more than White supremist groups claiming to be Christian should be attributed to all of Christianity.[4]

---

[3] Anderson E. (2022). Black in white space: The enduring impact of color in everyday life. University of Chicago Press.
https://doi.org/10.7208/chicago/9780226815176.001.0001
[4] Hoffman, L., Granger, N., Jr., Vallejos, L., & Moats, M. (2016). An existential-humanistic perspective on Black Lives Matter and contemporary protest movements. *Journal of Humanistic Psychology, 56*(6), 595–611.

Be BRAVER

Breathe. If you are new to the terminologies presented above, take another breath. If you have previously argued against the concepts of white privilege and white spaces, please take another breath. If you are a Black, Indigenous, person of color, take a big breath and exhale as fully as you are able. And again. **Reflect** on what your responses are right now. Which phrase caught your attention the most? What surprised you in this section? What do you want more information about? What questions do you have about the terminology used? What needs clarification? **Accept** it all. Be open to all that is showing up in your body. Feel and name your emotions. Notice what happens when you do that. What might be **vulnerable** and risky to voice right now? **Engage** with your curiosity. If you're reading this with others, what would be the optimal outcome of this conversation? What do you need in this moment? **Reflect** on this experience. What did you learn about yourself and/or others in this conversation?

The protection of white space is intricately linked to the phrase "Black Lives Matter." The hashtag of #blacklivesmatter originated after 17-year-old Trayvon Martin was shot and killed in Sanford, Florida in 2012 by a neighborhood watch volunteer, George Zimmerman. Upon seeing the young man in a "hoodie," Zimmerman assumed that the young man was involved in a recent robbery in the area, called for police backup and attempted to make a citizen's arrest. In the ensuing altercation, Zimmerman fatally shot Martin in the chest.

I happen to live about forty minutes away from Sanford. It's where my hay supplier is located, so I go there on a regular basis. A semi-rural community on the outskirts of Orlando, Sanford also happened to be a popular campaign and rally stop for President Trump before, during, and after his presidential term. For me, every trip to Sanford comes with trepidation and the awareness of the white space I'm stepping into. During the height of the global pandemic and anti-Chinese rhetoric, my embodied experience was one of hypervigilance for potential altercations each time I set foot in the feed store, face mask in place to hide my fear, while simultaneously drawing attention to my existence as "other" in an anti-mask environment. Even with all that, I understand that my presence as an Asian woman in white spaces is less life threatening than for many of my Black friends.

There are numerous examples of what happens when Black lives are seen in white spaces. The automatic assumption that they are trespassing, and by association breaking the law in some way, has led to many altercations with law enforcement and members of these white spaces who perceive themselves as victims of a crime being committed, resulting in the death of many Black lives.

The equine industry is undoubtedly a white space. In some disciplines, in particular, it is distinctly an elitist white space. In talking to other Black, Indigenous, and people of color within the equine industry, I cannot count the number of stories I've heard about the suspicion that is aroused by our presence. From being asked outright whether we are authorized to be at a facility (as the owner of the facility), to having the police called for trespassing during a horse show while attempting to return to our own trailers, it is clear that we are not welcome by virtue of our skin color.

The time has come for change.

Elizabeth McCorvey is a licensed social worker and equine-facilitated practitioner who also offers anti-oppressive training to mental health practitioners. We've shared our experiences with each other about how our presence in these spaces disrupts people's perceptions and opinions about Black, Indigenous, and people of color. Since the 2020 protests surrounding the death of George Floyd, we have both been buoyed by the number of invitations we have received for interviews and presentations on the topic of diversity, equity, and inclusion. Organizations such as the American Horse Council, PATH International, in both their national and regional divisions, the Therapeutic Riding Association of Virginia, are among those who have actively engaged with these issues. I am hopeful that things are changing, but the work cannot all be done by people of color. We need white folks to walk alongside us in this fight; to do the work of looking inward to root out the unconscious biases; to feel offended when we are offended so that we don't have to carry the full burden on our backs.

The first step is to acknowledge the reality of white privilege and white spaces. A dear friend of mine and I had a conversation recently about what it means to be seen. Truly seen. Not the type of seeing that means that you notice another's presence, but the type of seeing that is actively engaged and intentional. For me, this type of being seen comes with a feeling of spaciousness, an opening that I can step into. Perhaps it's something to do with the prolonged social distancing measures of recent times, but even as I write this I can feel the yearning for stepping into open arms and being embraced with warmth and gladness on my arrival. It's the difference between opening the door for someone to step inside and waiting with the door open and rushing to greet them with pleasure.

This is an important distinction in the complexities of the current racial discourse. Because agreeing with the phrase Black Lives Matter is simply the bare *minimum*. Cultivating a space where Black lives are welcomed, respected, encouraged, beloved, and cherished is what is really needed. But in a world where we are still arguing over whether Black lives matter, this often feels like a steep mountain to climb.

For those of you who want to stand up for racial justice, I want to encourage you to build an awareness of how and when you can do more than the minimum. What might you change to be more welcoming to Black, Indigenous, and people of color? What do you respect, encourage, cherish, and love? How might you be more intentional in how you engage with folks who feel marginalized because of the color of their skin? How might you advocate and promote their work? What are you doing to support yourself in these difficult conversations with others in the majority so that you can truly advocate for inclusion? How does this translate from an individual intentional practice to an organizational or community- wide commitment? Whether you are joining book clubs to discuss the anti-racist work by Black authors, or joining social activist groups, or donating to Black Lives Matter, or supporting Black businesses, let's bring these conversations into our industry. And if you're not doing any of those things, what's stopping you?

Within the field of equine-facilitated work, what are we doing as leaders of training organizations, equine-facilitated learning programs, therapeutic centers, and private practices to increase access to our offerings to Black communities? The HERD Institute is committed to bringing more diversity into our field and working on funding more programs and training opportunities. But that's just the bare minimum. How can we build a culture of inclusion so that those we want to welcome into this space actually feel like they belong and not feel out of place? I know how it feels to be the only person of color in the room. I also know how excited I get when I see others who look like me. And I'm aware of how seldom that happens.

In our conversation, I was moved to tears when my friend said, "I promise not only to see you, but to look for you." This commitment to look for those who may be under-represented in any space resonated with my desire to cultivate a more diverse and inclusive community. So,

I am actively looking. For those of you who identify as Black, Indigenous, people of color, I am looking for you, and I am eagerly awaiting your arrival and will meet you with open arms.

Chapter 15

Racial Microaggressions

Microaggressions, both verbal and non-verbal, happen all the time. They can be defined as verbal or non-verbal, slights or insults that are often unintentional, and where the person delivering them is unaware of the harm or offense caused.[1]

To the woman in line at the check-out this morning[2]:

It was sweet of you to strike up a conversation with me this morning as we waited in line. I saw the surprise on your face when I started to speak. Your eyebrows furrowed and your forehead crinkled while you tilted your head to the side in your attempt to focus your listening. You smiled at me then and told me slowly that I speak English well, before asking me where I am from.

You may have noticed my body turning away from you in response to your compliment, and perhaps I may have stepped away from you slightly. You might even have noticed that when I replied that I'm from England, that this came with a tight-lipped smile. I turned my back to you then in the hope that you might pick up from these subtle signs that I was disengaging from our conversation. You see, it wasn't that I didn't want to shoot the breeze with you, or that I didn't hear your compliment, it's just that I knew that what would follow would leave me feeling dejected.

I guess you didn't notice this though because your curiosity about what/who I am and where I might fit into your pre-existing pigeonholes motivated you enough to ask me whether I'd learned to speak English there or in the USA. At this point, you may have noticed me taking a deep breath while simultaneously stiffening my neck. The deep breath was to

---

[1] Sue, D. W., & Spanierman, L. (2020). *Microaggressions in everyday life.* Wiley.

[2] Lac, V. (2015, March 5) I know you think you're complimenting me, but you're not. *New Existentialists.* Retrieved from https://www.saybrook.edu/2015/03/24/03-24-15/

help me calm myself internally, giving me time to remind myself that your ignorance is not your fault, that you don't know what you don't know, and that based on past experiences, confronting such ignorance with defensiveness or anger would likely make matters worse. The stiffening in my neck was my catching myself in my body movements to avoid shaking my head in disbelief. You know, the way you might do when you get really confused and need a reality check, so you shake your head in the hope that it clears things up when you open your eyes again. But I knew that shaking my head wouldn't help matters, and I didn't want to appear rude, so I refrained from following through with what my body instinctively wanted to do.

I'm not sure what happened for you next when I repeated that I'm from England, so yes that's where I learned to speak. You appeared even more baffled by me and looked at me as if I were an alien. You asked me, "Do they speak English there then?" At which point I was enormously grateful that my turn in line had come and I was able to extricate myself from our conversation, but not before telling you that this conversation was confusing me now. You looked hurt and confused and muttered something about how you were just trying to be nice.

Nice?

No. You weren't being nice. You were being inquisitive out of ignorance. I'm actually okay with that. We don't know what we don't know, and we all suffer from a level of ignorance. But you weren't being "nice." You didn't mean to be rude or condescending, and it wasn't your intention to irritate or upset me. I know that, too. When you said I speak English well, I know you meant it as a compliment. This doesn't mean that it actually is one. The implication is that I am a foreigner and it's a surprise to you that I know how to speak English, let alone speak it well. Your surprise tells me more about you than you realize. It tells me that you are not aware of your white privilege. It tells me that you have never had to think about what it means to be white. It tells me that you live in a homogenous world with very narrow horizons. I'm pretty sure you weren't actually asking me if English people speak English, although if you were, I think that would be a whole other level of ignorance that I'm not sure I could actually get my head around. I'm guessing you meant to ask if Chinese people in England also speak English, or something to that effect.

To you, our interaction and your experience of me this morning was probably something novel and maybe a little amusing. I imagine you went home and thought nothing more of it, other than maybe wonder why I was so abrupt with you when you were just trying to make conversation.

What you don't know is how much these kinds of interactions are everyday reminders of my yearning to just belong and be accepted for who I am, without having to justify my existence. Sometimes, I can muster the patience to be polite in these encounters, and other times I just find them bone-weary exhausting.

I can understand if you think I'm being over dramatic and/or over sensitive. I can also understand if you might be confused by how I have turned a friendly conversation and your genuine curiosity into something so loaded. I know that you don't get it.

Here's the thing—just because you don't get it, it doesn't mean that it's okay. Just because you don't get it, doesn't mean that it's not real. Just because you don't get it, doesn't mean that I won't desperately want you to understand. But what I really want you to know is that in my attempt to do that, I might lose my cool and I hope you can handle that gracefully. Because, quite frankly, if I am drawing on all my reserves to engage in a difficult conversation with you about what it means to be a person of color living in a white suburban space, I need you to find some compassion. It's the same level of compassion that I attempted to dig up during our conversation this morning. Without accessing my compassion toward you, I would have lashed out and ranted at you for your ignorance. I could have taken your ignorance and ascribed it as a trait of all white Americans and washed my hands of the whole situation by telling myself that there is no solution for such parochialism. Without accessing my compassion toward myself, I would have berated myself for not having enough energy to just go along with the conversation and thank you for complimenting my English.

So please, dig deep and find your compassion for those who are different to you by asking yourself: What do you take for granted by living in a world where everyone looks, sounds, and behaves the same as you? What if you didn't have that sameness and sense of belonging? I urge you to please find that compassion within yourself to acknowledge that what you think is "nice" might actually be unintentionally offensive, and what you think is a compliment is loaded with privileged assumptions. So, forgive me for not accepting your comment as a compliment, because it really wasn't one.

With hope for a more compassionate approach to difference,
The British Chinese woman who confused you this morning.

Be BRAVER

Breathe. Reflect. Accept. Vulnerable. Engage. Reflect.

By this point, I'm hoping that you need fewer prompts to practice being BRAVER. I'm curious about what your reaction was in reading this scenario. What surprised you? What piqued your interest? What about this situation made you feel vulnerable? How might you have engaged with me in that moment if you were this woman? What might you have said? What would you have done differently?

Another aspect of white privilege is that when faced with the type of scenario above, as a person of color, I am always mindful of the need to not offend when calling someone out, *even if I am offended*. This necessitates an enormous amount of effort to dampen my anger, swallow it down, and dig deep for compassion to respond in a way that doesn't leave me being labeled as the "angry person of color who is playing the race card," something that white folks are never accused of. Since these types of conversations occur on a regular basis, there exists a collective physical toll on people of color carrying these burdens.

Racial trauma and race-based stress can be defined as the cumulative effects of physical, mental, and emotional stress and injury resulting from interactions with racial bias and discrimination at individualized, organizational, or societal levels. These experiences can have significant psychological and physiological effects and can result in symptoms similar to those who suffer with post-traumatic stress disorder (PTSD). While my interaction with the woman at the check-out was not an overtly racialized encounter, these unintentional slights, or microaggressions, form a significant proportion of the types of cumulative racial trauma that Black, Indigenous, and people of color face every single day.

Intersectionality

While I have focused on racial injustice and racial microaggressions, it's important to note that microaggressions are experienced by all marginalized folk. Racism, sexism, ableism (to encompass cognitive and physical), sizeism, ageism, homophobia, transphobia, xenophobia, anti-Semitism, and other forms of religious discrimination, are all catalysts for microaggressions.

Most of us will occupy some intersectionality in our lives with experiences of being a part of the majority while also holding a marginalized position. You may be part of a dominant culture as a white man who holds a marginalized position in living with a physical disability. You may be a Black cisgender, heterosexual man with no awareness of the struggles of a white gay man. My experience as an Asian woman will be vastly different from the experiences of my friend, Maggie, who is a cisgender, heterosexual, Black woman from Zambia. Her experiences will be different to those of Elizabeth, who is a cisgender, queer, Black woman born in the United States. We may resonate with each other on many levels, but our positionalities are distinct. What we categorically can share are our experiences of microaggressions.

The problem with microaggressions is that they often leave the recipient feeling discombobulated. Since many microaggressions occur when folks holding a majority position are offering what they intend as a compliment, what happens for the marginalized person is a complex process to resist internal gaslighting. By this, I mean that it sends us into an internal process that sounds a bit like this: Am I overreacting? Should I let that one go? Don't be so sensitive. But that hurt. Is this a relationship that is worth investing the energy in to call them out? Is it safe? Are they going to get defensive if I do? Will I offend them? Maybe I shouldn't say anything. Oh, but it feels so icky. I have to say something. Okay, tread carefully. That makes me so angry that I'm the one that has to not offend, even though they offended me! Okay, slow down, calm down.

This internal dialogue happens every time I'm faced with a microaggression. Every time. They're micro-aggressions. So, I'm not even talking about intentionally offensive, aggressive physical or verbal racial assaults, although I've experienced those, too. I'm talking about when I'm with my friends and colleagues doing everyday things. Examples of microaggressions I receive most often include:

1) You don't look like how you sound.
2) Where are you really from?
3) I don't see you as Asian.

Let me break down why these phrases are considered to be microaggressions and how they are intricately linked to white majority standards and expectations. First, I don't look like how I sound. What does that mean? For those of you who have met me in person and experienced the same surprise, please know that I get that you're surprised. It's *why* you are surprised that stings. Is your surprise rooted in the expectation for people who look like me to speak in broken English? Is your surprise based on the expectation that you thought I would speak in an American accent? Your surprise tells me that your worldview does not include enough difference to assimilate, without being startled, the possibility that there are Black, Indigenous, and people of color around the world who speak English fluently without an American accent.

If you stop to think about it, it's pretty obvious that there are millions of people around the world who speak in the languages of the country they were born and/or raised in. If my speaking in an English accent blows your mind, wait till I tell you about my husband's cousins who grew up speaking Swedish and Danish! They're Asian too.

Now, I know that this is an unconscious bias, so the first time you tell me that I don't look like how I sound, I can let it go. But, so often, I am told this repeatedly, and after a while, it gets old. Each time you tell me that, it's yet another reminder that I don't belong. And if we dig a little deeper, this phrase often goes hand in hand with the comment that I speak English well. The assumption in that is that because I'm not white, I won't be articulate. I hear this backhanded compliment bestowed upon so many of my friends who are Black, Indigenous, and people of color, but not once have I ever heard this praise delivered from one white American to another. Ever. Why is that? The historical subjugation of Black, Indigenous, and people of color has resulted in the unconscious expectation from white society that we are inferior. The message that has been passed down through the generations is that by virtue of not being white, we are less intelligent, less productive, less successful. The historically white space of the media has perpetuated stereotypes of gang culture and illiteracy for Black and Latinx populations. Indigenous people are stereotyped as unreliable alcoholics. The list of stereotypes goes on.

Practice Being BRAVER

Let's take a moment here to practice our skills of being BRAVER
Breathe. Reflect. Accept. Vulnerable. Engage. Reflect.

Please allow me to reiterate that this book isn't about blaming and shaming anyone. My aim is to increase our collective awareness of what happens in these types of interactions, where we feel it in our bodies, and find a way forward with intention. I want to point out that I have also had Asian Americans comment on my accent, so there's an added layer of internalized racism that's happening. And while I sometimes get irritated by these comments, I do understand your surprise. It's human nature to have these biases.

This brings us to the second question that I get all the time: "Where are you really from?" Of course, it's natural to inquire of new acquaintances where they come from. When I'm in the company of white Americans, I've noticed how accepting everyone is when someone says something like, "I'm from New York," or "I'm from Pittsburgh but I live in Chicago." There's usually some kind of reference associated with sports teams, and I've learned over the years that if someone says they're from Columbus, Ohio, that it's a perfectly welcomed response to shout "O-H" and receive the reply of "I-O" in return. I've also learned that when it comes to my turn to answer the question, I'm often subjected to multiple rounds. Apparently, "I'm from the UK" doesn't quite cut it. "Oh", they'll say, "but where are you *actually* from?" I would be willing to bet that every single one of my Asian friends will have been asked that question at some point, even if they were born in the United States.

I want to be clear that I am not advocating for everyone to walk on eggshells for fear of being offensive. Nor am I proposing some kind of extreme political correctness. What I am suggesting is the need to be more mindful about the impact of questions like these, and perhaps find an alternative way of getting to know your new neighbor/work colleague/social acquaintance. In my mind, my "perfect" stranger might ask me "Where do you call home?"

"I Don't See Color"

I've lost count of the number of times people have told me that they don't see me as Chinese or Asian. The irony is that this often comes from people who also initially commented on how I don't sound like how I look when they first meet me. Somehow, over time, the cognitive dissonance they experienced at the beginning is replaced by a need to put aside differences. Remember, a sense of belonging is cultivated through feeling accepted as all of who we are, not through a process of fitting in. Which begs the question, if you don't see me as Asian, what do you see me as? And why is it so important to you to not see color, and discount my differences?

During high school and college, I made friends with folks from diverse backgrounds. Perhaps we were all drawn to one another with our shared experiences of being different, but my friends group included Chinese, Trinidadian, Japanese, Korean, Nigerian, Zambian, Gambian, and Bahraini folks. Whenever I mentioned my friends to my dad, particularly if we were with his peers, he would declare proudly that "my daughter is colorblind," a testament to my transnational upbringing. I struggled to explain that it wasn't that I was colorblind, but that it was precisely the opposite—that I found kinship with others who stood out from the white space that we existed within. It wasn't that we treated each other as though we were all the same. We treated each other with respect for our cultural differences, acknowledging that we're *not* the same. It was in the acceptance of differences that brought us together, where we felt seen and supported.

I know that for many years, it was deemed to be progressive to be colorblind. In many ways, the intention to not see color was an attempt at addressing political incorrectness and racial injustice. But we live and learn. If we pause to consider what not seeing color means, we can easily identify why this is problematic. When someone says, "I don't see color and I treat everyone the same," I'm always left with the inclination to ask, "The same as what or whom?" What is the measure of sameness, really? The same as other white people who look like you? Or the same as other people who look like me? And if the measure of sameness is of other white people, does that mean there's an implicit acknowledgment that you know not everyone is treated equally? And what if that sameness doesn't fit everyone? You see? This inquisitive mind of mine can't help asking those questions which all boil down to the reality that differences exist and we cannot pretend that they don't.

Let's take a real-life example from within the equine industry that has been gaining much needed attention of late. I think it provides a useful illustration of how saying "I don't see color" is problematic and dangerous. The issue of properly fitted helmets and the lack of inclusion that traditional helmets offer has been emerging in the last few years. For those of you who offer therapeutic riding lessons and/or typical riding lessons, what do you do when a child comes into the barn for a lesson? I know that one of the first things I do is to fit the child for a helmet. I also know that one of the challenges when I'm fitting helmets for a Black child is that these helmets aren't designed for Black hair. This results in helmets that are improperly fitted, increasing the risk of injury for the child. Shelly Watts, CEO of Muirneen Equestrian, a body positive and inclusive equestrian clothing brand, along with Caitlin Gooch, a Black equestrian, author, and Founder of Saddle up and Read, have been campaigning helmet manufacturers and asking some challenging questions.

This "I don't see color" and "treating everyone the same" philosophy from helmet manufacturers means that Black equestrians are faced with the choice of not wearing a helmet or making do with ill-fitting ones. Sameness in this context is the assumption that all hair types are suitably catered to by existing helmet designs. A counterargument for this dilemma is for Black riders to change their hairstyles (without acknowledgment of the cultural significance of natural hair) to fit the helmet, and thereby highlighting the point that sameness often equates to whitewashing. Additionally, by assuming that there are no differences, we ignore the increased risks associated with improperly fitted helmets for Black equestrians. How is this treating everyone the same? If we dig a little deeper, now that manufacturers are aware of the issue, what steps are being taken to address this? At what point does it become clear that Black lives matter less if the issue is not addressed?

"I Just Can't Get it Right"

At the 2022 PATH International Annual Conference, I was asked to take part in the opening panel discussion on diversity, equity, and inclusion. The panel included Kathy Alm (CEO), a couple of PATH International members, and members from the DEI Committee; it was moderated by Michael Kaufmann, the then Chair of the committee. During the discussion, a theme emerged of how difficult it is to say the right thing in conversations around diversity and inclusion, and a general fear of being attacked/hurt even if coming from good intentions. As I listened to my fellow panelists and audience comments, I desperately wanted to offer something that would be relatable to them. Once again, my relationship with horses came to my aid. I asked the audience for a show of hands if they had ever fallen off a horse. The majority of the 400+ attendees raised their hands. I asked them how many of them had fallen off more than once. The hands stayed up. I asked them how many of them had given up riding because they'd had a fall and been hurt/injured. Every hand dropped. I asked them how many of us would be here now if we gave up because we didn't get it right with our horse, and if there was something that we could learn from that to take into our conversations about diversity, equity, and inclusion. I want to invite you to consider this, too.

I recognize that what we're talking about here is nuanced and complex and that we won't get it right all the time. I include myself in that. I'm also aware that it might seem like a contradiction to ask that you see me for my differences while also being mindful of not treating me as "other" in the microaggressions that we've mentioned. As always, these conversations need to be situated within the context of relationships. The paradoxical nature of this process is that with increased self-awareness of microaggressions, we can lean more fully into authentic ways of relating, become more open and tolerant of differences, and cultivate a more inclusive environment for all.

Being BRAVER

Breathe. Reflect. How do you feel reading this? **Accept** whatever comes up. What feels **vulnerable** and risky? **Engage** with what you need right now. **Reflect.** What are you taking away from this experience?

Chapter 16

Other Microaggressions

It doesn't interest me what you do for a living. I want to know what you ache for, and if you dare to dream of meeting your heart's longing."
~ Oriah Mountain Dreamer[1]

Microaggressions are not limited to racial biases. They show up in all kinds of ways in our daily conversations based on assumptions and unconscious beliefs that we have assimilated from our daily lives. I finally realized why I hate small talk. I'm a therapist. I like getting down and dirty, delving into the nitty gritty of what makes us human, and feeling a deep connection with whomever I'm with. I'm uncomfortable with the superficiality and triteness of small talk.

As an existential and depth therapist, I'm accustomed to listening to the woes of the world and am privy to details from the underbelly of human existence. I sit with the existential dilemmas that face my clients, all while attempting to maintain a sense of awe and wonder at the beauty of life. But small talk irks me because it isn't always small. Instead, small talk has the potential to bring up deep, dark, painful issues and isn't a safe place for them to be explored, and these deep issues probably don't belong in conversations with complete strangers or newly made acquaintances.

We've explored some of the nuances behind some racial microaggressions, but let's look more broadly at some other examples of seemingly innocent questions that reveal other unconscious biases in our society. These seemingly innocuous questions are almost always part of any social gathering:

1) Are you married?
2) Do you have children? How many?

---

[1] Mountain Dreamer, O. (1999) *The invitation*. HarperCollins.

Nothing wrong with those questions, surely? They're perfectly normal questions to ask someone you've just met, right? How can any of them be insulting or hurtful? Let's take a closer look.

Are You Married?

Personally, yes. This one isn't painful for me, but what about those who are going through a divorce, or those who aren't married but would like to be? A friend of mine is repeatedly asked why she isn't married yet and when she's going to find a nice man to settle down with, questions that clearly impose values predicated on a system of patriarchy that a woman's worth is inextricably tied to her ability to find a husband. Add to that, the question of whether one is married is steeped in heteronormativity. What if I was gay, lesbian, bisexual or transgender? Is this the time to come out to someone I've just met? Is it safe to do so, or might I be in danger of being ostracized, or worse? The emotional burden for LGBTQIA folks to constantly navigate the potential trauma of either being outed, or outing themselves, is persistent and well documented, but let's add another layer to this conversation. With the enactment of the "Don't Say Gay" legislation in Florida, a teacher meeting with parents at a school fundraiser social event and engaging in some general chit chat now brings additional anxieties for an LGBTQIA-identifying teacher. What happens if the parents don't want their children to know that their teacher has a same-sex spouse? Those who identify as heterosexual have the liberty to talk about our partners and spouses without fear of retaliation. What if this teacher accidentally mentions his husband when speaking with a student? What might be the consequences of that in Florida now?

Working with organizations wanting to increase diversity, equity, and inclusion in their workforce, I have been asked on numerous occasions why it's necessary to bring sexual orientation and identity into the workplace. Comments such as "I'm not homophobic, and I don't care what people do behind closed doors, but why do I need to hear about it?" prioritize the easing of discomfort for the majority over creating an inclusive space for marginalized people. Annual celebrations during PRIDE month are often a source of discomfort.

Being BRAVER

Breathe. Reflect. How do you feel reading this? **Accept** whatever comes up. What feels **vulnerable** and risky? **Engage** with what you need right now. **Reflect.** What are you taking away from this experience?

Do You Have Children?

For many people, being childless is not a choice. It is a painful journey of hope and despair. Infertility rates are increasing, and research shows that infertility is one of the primary reasons for divorce among couples. Assisted reproduction has increased in the United States as people are choosing to start families later in life. This means that the chances of having a miscarriage and or an unsuccessful fertility treatment cycle are also rising. Nearly 41% of women suffering from infertility have depression as they experience a lack of self-worth in their inability to bear a child.

As someone who has experienced infertility, it always surprises me how my answer to this question always leads to further probing. If someone tells you that they don't have children, your follow-up questions about whether they want them, or if they're trying or planning to, are boorish, particularly if you've just met. Even worse, telling someone that they still have time (because they're still young) is painful and invasive. Even if I had intentionally chosen to be childless, like many people I know, this question places an expectation for me to justify *why* I might be childless. Which, frankly, is still not something I am obliged to share and is none of your business. I have witnessed the dilemma among those who have lost children of answering truthfully or superficially. One friend particularly struggles when asked how many children she has as she lost her first child through a stillbirth, but now has two toddlers and another on the way. Does she say that she has four without opening the door to more questions that lead to revealing her horror? Another has had multiple pregnancies that all resulted in stillbirths. Can she say that she feels like she has children without explaining her painful reality and reliving her trauma? There are so many assumptions at play in this inquiry based on society's expectations that women should have children.

The current political climate in the United States is such that the topic of children has the potential to naturally segue into a discussion about the recent Supreme Court's decision to overturn Roe v. Wade and the increasing restrictions on women's rights to access abortions. These conversations are emotive and are inextricably linked to social justice, particularly since Supreme Court Justice Clarence Thomas stated in his concurring opinion that considering this ruling, the Supreme Court should also reconsider legislation regarding access to contraception as well as same-sex marriage. Given the health disparities already discussed, historically marginalized populations will once again bear the burden of harm from these legislative measures.

Being BRAVER

Breathe. Reflect. How do you feel reading this? **Accept** whatever comes up. What feels **vulnerable** and risky? **Engage** with what you need right now. **Reflect.** What are you taking away from this experience?

I repeat: I am not advocating for folks to walk on eggshells for fear of being offensive. My aim is to offer insight into the impact of seemingly innocuous comments. Yes, this takes effort, and we'll make mistakes as we navigate alternative ways to engage in social interactions. Sometimes it's not the opening questions that are the most hurtful, but the responses and opinions offered. Flippant comments or opinions during small talk often acts to deflect from any awkwardness felt from receiving an unexpected answer. Avoiding awkwardness doesn't make insensitivity acceptable.

Despite my aversion to small talk, I recognize that it can be an important way of beginning the journey toward friendship, so perhaps we can find ways to make that experience more enjoyable for each other. Much of the hurtful impact of small talk is in the cultural biases and prejudices that we all hold. How we respond depends on our cultural identity and sense of belonging, as well as other personal experiences that might make one topic more painful than others.

During the holiday season every year, I find myself agonizing over the impending holiday parties that I am obliged to attend with my husband. I joke that I must put my "corporate wife hat" on to smile and nod at people at these gatherings that are often too loud and crowded for me. I prepare myself emotionally before these events by reminding myself that it's only a few hours of small talk, and I have the internal resources to get through it in one piece. I have my stock answers prepared for the most likely questions, and I can always hide in the restroom if I need a break.

Last year, as part of my preparations for the holiday season, I shared my trepidations with my friends Elizabeth and Alison. I wondered if there was an alternative way to engage in conversations at these events that didn't involve me bracing myself and, instead, lean in with curiosity. Alison, astute as ever, asked me what I was missing in these events that stopped me from bringing myself more authentically, rather than feeling like I had a role to play. Elizabeth, creative as always, offered me a series of one-liners and dramatic conversation starters to help entertain me in the process. I realized that my struggle was less about wanting to protect myself from potential microaggressions but more about a desire to connect and my own assumptions (biases) that I wouldn't be able to find that within this space, and that I wouldn't belong. Elizabeth gently suggested that perhaps instead of holding my sense of not belonging on my own, I could look around the room during the event for others who might be standing alone and ask if I could join them. This simple strategy allowed me to do what I do best—look for others who might need support and create a feeling of inclusion—while also creating support for myself. "My friend suggested that I look for others who might be on their own if I was feeling out of place tonight. May I join you?" has now been beta tested at multiple events. Not only did it bring a feeling of camaraderie in the moment with the person I approached, but when overheard by someone else, allowed them to ask if they could join in, too.

I realized in this process that small talk can be used as either a buffer to keep your distance or as an invitation to the other for stepping into your life. It can be a way for perfect strangers to become friends. It makes sense that we often begin by trying to find something in common with the person we've just met. But my experience is that this leads to a rapid categorization full of assumptions of the person we are with, which distances us from each other. Rather than running down a standard checklist of questions, maybe we can look for a more inclusive way to find out more about the person we are with. Maybe, we can open the door for connection by simply saying, "It's lovely to meet you. Tell me about yourself."

Chapter 17

At Least the Others Are Normal

While working as a therapeutic riding instructor, like many of us doing this work, I had the joy of interacting with many families whose children presented with physical, cognitive, and emotional challenges. One of my students was an autistic boy who was non-speaking,[1] whom I had the pleasure of teaching for almost five years. When I first met him, he had very rigidly patterned behaviors. One of his routines meant that on arrival at the barn, he would run upstairs into the lounge area, run around the table three times in each direction, come back down and grab me by the face. He would then pull my head down toward him and sniff my entire face, pull back, and look into my eyes. This interaction with him was often the highlight of my week!

The first time he did this, his dad immediately tried to stop him. I told them both that it was fine, that this felt important somehow and happily received his greeting. Over the course of a year, this was his preferred greeting for me. Each time, I experienced this as an almost sacred ritual between us, and it gave me so much joy. It's hard for me to recall these moments without tearing up. It took me a while to figure out what he was doing, and my best guess is that he was imitating how the horses would greet him by sniffing. I truly believe that following his lead in this ritual allowed us to meet each other at a deeper level of connection. After a couple of years, these greetings became more infrequent. As he became less attached to his rigid patterns of behavior and his social skills broadened, he slowly replaced this face-sniffing ritual with high-fives and hugs.

In preparation for yet another upcoming relocation, I had stepped away from teaching for a couple of months. Prior to my move, I returned to the barn to say goodbye. I happened to arrive at the same time as this student's lesson began. As he walked up the driveway into the barn, he spotted me standing in the aisleway. His face broke out into the biggest

---

[1] I am using the term non-speaking rather than non-verbal to acknowledge that not all individuals who do not speak are incapable of understanding verbal language.

smile as he hurried over. By now, he had grown and was only a few inches shorter than I. He reached up toward my face, pulled me toward him, and sniffed all over my face, and then looked me deep in the eyes. "Thank you," I said, with tears in my eyes, "I needed that today. I'm going to miss you." In response, he grabbed my hand and led me toward the mounting block where his volunteer team and his horse were waiting. Leading me up onto the mounting block, it was clear that he wanted me to assist him to get on his horse. He held up one finger. "One last time, right?" I asked. He smiled as I helped him mount.

This student, and so many like him, are so often overlooked, misunderstood, and coerced into behaving in neurotypical ways. They are subjected to therapies that strip away their value and worth as neurodivergent individuals for the sake of conforming to what is deemed "normal." Their lived experiences of existing in a world that systematically oppresses the expression of those who do not fit the ideals of neurotypical behavior result in many autistic people being harmed in the process.

In my book *It's Not About the Activity: Thinking Outside the Toolbox in Equine Facilitated Psychotherapy & Learning,*[2] I emphasize the importance of meeting our clients and participants with respect, dignity, and compassion. Whether we are in the role of therapeutic riding instructor, equine specialist, educator, or therapist, we need to examine our own attitudes and implicit ableist perspectives to truly support those we serve. We need to listen to our neurodivergent colleagues, friends, and students when they tell us about the harm that they have experienced at the hands of those who had the best intentions but who didn't know better.

What is Neurodiversity?

Neurodiversity is the diversity of human brains and minds. It refers to the infinite variations in neurocognitive functioning within our species. There is a growing neurodiversity-affirmative movement that shares its roots with all social justice activism; that calls for a paradigm shift toward seeking civil rights, equality, respect, and full societal inclusion for the neurodivergent population. This means challenging the status quo of medicalized models and research that produces standards for what is considered "normal," and embracing the idea that

---

[2] Lac, V. (2020) *It's not about the activity: Thinking outside the toolbox in equine facilitated psychotherapy & learning.* University Professors Press.

neurodiversity is a natural and valuable form of human diversity. In parallel with other social justice movements that challenge racial, sexual, gender, age, and religious stereotypes, we need to debunk the idea that there is one "right" style of neurocognitive functioning, accept that this is a culturally constructed fiction—no more valid (and no more conducive to a healthy society or to the overall well-being of humanity) than the idea that there is one "normal" or "right" ethnicity, gender, or culture.

The term neurodivergent is used to refer to individuals whose cognitive functioning falls outside of the majority. These differences in cognitive functioning may be diagnosed as autism, dyslexia, dyspraxia, or attention-deficit/hyperactivity disorder, traumatic brain injury, drug addiction, or meditation practices. This is not an exhaustive list of the types of neurodivergent functioning that exist.

In contrast, those individuals who fall within the parameters of societal expectations of neurological functioning are deemed to be neurotypical. As with any majority/minority dynamic, the social dynamics that manifest regarding neurodiversity are like those of other forms of human diversity, where neurodivergent individuals may often experience prejudice, misunderstanding, and/or oppression from society's neurotypical majority. Steve Silberman, author of *Neurotribes: The legacy of autism and the future of neurodiversity,* says that neurodiversity "should be regarded as naturally occurring cognitive variations with distinctive strengths that have contributed to the evolution of technology and culture rather than as mere checklists of deficits and dysfunctions."[3] So rather than working toward eliminating these differences, we need to embrace them.

One of my clients is a father of three elementary-school-aged children. His eldest daughter is 8, his middle daughter is 7, and his son is 5. His wife died of COVID-19 complications after being hospitalized at the start of the pandemic, and he has been struggling with his grief while trying to raise his family. His son was diagnosed with autism when he was 3 years old, and while he attends various therapies and has access to support, their daily lives are challenging. The father started therapy after an altercation with a stranger at the local supermarket. In his first session, he described a scenario that I'm sure looks all too familiar to many parents attempting to corral their children while grocery shopping. Except his son was experiencing

---

[3] Silberman S. (2015). *Neurotribes: The legacy of autism and the future of neurodiversity.* Avery an imprint of Penguin Random House.

sensory overload. The fluorescent light in the aisle was flashing intermittently, and it pushed his son over his window of tolerance for external stimulus. The father decided to abandon his shopping cart to attend to his son by picking him up and carrying him out of the store, while his daughters trailed behind. As he walked toward the exit, he could feel the eyes of strangers on him, shaking their heads in judgment. A woman walked by muttering, "I hope you're not going to let him get away with that behavior." He stopped in his tracks. "He's autistic; what's your excuse?" he snapped. "Oh, I'm sorry," she replied. "Well, at least the others are normal."

Being BRAVER

Breathe. Reflect. Accept. Vulnerable. Engage. Reflect.

What are you experiencing right now? How easy is it to accept your feelings about this scenario? How does it compare with previous exercises? If it's easier, what makes it so? If not, what's difficult? What are you curious about? What do you want to engage with? What are you taking from this experience?

Non-judgment and Authenticity

I have often been asked if I am neurodivergent by those who identify as such themselves. I've wondered about that myself but have never felt the need to be assessed and receive a formal diagnosis. I do know that I connect deeply and easily to neurodivergent folks and seem to have an in-built shorthand of how we communicate with each other. When I look at the diagnostic criteria and assessment tools used for autism, there are numerous traits that I recognize: my obsessive nature; auditory, tactile, and light sensitivity; and how my brain processes macro and micro data simultaneously, to name a few. Whether I view these traits from a medical model framework or from an existential–humanistic perspective, I know that part of the reason why I feel an affinity to neurodivergent people is because it's one of the safest communities I have experienced being in. My felt sense when I am in the presence of a neurodivergent-affirming group is that I can be transparent and authentic with all my quirkiness and still be accepted.

There's an effortlessness to being with others who know what it's like to hide parts of themselves. Rather than trying to mask our differences, to show up with them and recognize that we are not alone brings me so much joy and relief. There's something about being in a space where acceptance and inclusion are offered without the need to prove yourself first.

For me, this is where the horses come in. I've worked with different breeds of horses in different countries, different facilities, and different riding disciplines. I used to board my horse at a facility with a diverse range of horses that included off-the-track thoroughbreds, dressage, showjumping, and three-day-eventing horses through to Western reining, cutting, trail horses, and regular riding school and 4-H ponies, as well as therapeutic riding horses. Some of the horses came with distinguished bloodlines and heavy price tags; others were show champions with multiple trophies. Some had never competed or were rescued from slaughter. The beauty of all this diversity is that while we might associate the three-day-eventer horse with his rich, Ivy-League educated, corporate lawyer owner, and the therapeutic riding horse with the non-profit organization run by volunteers, when the horses are grazing in the fields with one another none of that is relevant because the human-centric values that we have placed on these horses are not important *to them*.

We often talk about horses as being non-judgmental. We offer this as the reason why equine-facilitated work can be so powerful. We bear witness to those moments of connection between our clients and our horses when human value judgments are not present. But, when people tell me that horses are great to work with because they are non-judgmental, I become cautious. I question the validity of this because we are ascribing a human-centric concept to our horses. I wonder what it is that we really mean when we say that they are non-judgmental. Is it that we don't share the same social codes of morality? Is it that we are speaking different languages, so any judgments are lost in translation? Do we mean that they don't show that they have an opinion of what our clients are saying? I know that my horses have clear opinions and preferences for how I show up in relation to them, and they will respond if I challenge the status quo of how things are routinely done. Does this mean that they are "judging" me for my actions? Maybe not in the human-centric value-based understanding of judgment, but since freedom, choice, and consent are embedded into the way that we work with our horses at The HERD Institute, they are able to authentically *respond*.

In a similar way, I also don't subscribe to the idea that horses are "mirrors"—an idea that is prevalent within the equine-facilitated world, indicating that horses will often act as we feel in the moment. For example, if I'm scared the horses will mirror my fear. Of what we now know about nervous system dysregulation and co-regulation, wouldn't it be more accurate to say that horses *respond and react* to the energy and emotions we bring into the interaction? That they are, in fact, engaging in a relational way of being and offering feedback within the relationship? If they are simply "mirrors," aren't we reducing them to a tool for narcissistic reflection and missing the nuanced relational moments that may be available within the interaction? If they are "mirrors," aren't we also reducing them to a stereotype and generalization of how horses are expected to behave? Where then, does this leave the countless interactions I believe we have all witnessed when the horses respond in a way that is counter to this framework; when they have helped to down-regulate a highly distressed client by being steadfast and grounded in the presence of human struggles?

I ask these questions not to be pedantic but to bring attention to the impact of these perceptions and the parallels they pose in human interactions within the context of our understanding of diversity, equity, and inclusion, and particularly societal understanding of neurodiversity. I believe that it is critical to maintain humility in acknowledging that we don't have all the answers; that it is by virtue of recognizing the unknown that we can deepen our understanding; and that necessitates asking questions from viewpoints that are outside of the majority. I appreciate how challenging it is to step outside of the status quo. This is evident even in the etymology of the term *neurodivergent*, which prioritizes a medical-model-brain development perspective over a holistic view of the human experience through an integration of body and mind. Language matters. It is a product of the prevailing culture, revealing societal perceptions and practices, while simultaneously influencing public policy and research directions.

Within the field of existential–humanistic psychology, we have critiqued the basis of the DSM-5[4] as being culturally biased, lacking in scientific basis, pathologizing human experiences, and promoting a pharmaceutical approach to treatment. My colleagues within the Society for Humanistic Psychology, Division 32 of the American Psychological Association—Brent Dean Robbins, Sarah Kamens, and

---

[4] American Psychiatric Association (2022). The diagnostic and statistical manual of mental disorders (revised 5th ed.). American Psychiatric Association.

David Elkins led the charge in 2011 by publishing an Open Letter to petition the publication of the manual.[5] This Open Letter received endorsements from over 50 national and international organizations, and the petition was signed by over 15,000 people. I see these efforts as evidence of the momentum that has been building to challenge the status quo and offer alternatives on perspectives of human suffering. At the Global Summit on Diagnostic Alternatives in 2013, Sarah Kamens and colleagues articulated their mission statement by saying,

> *Something new is happening in the world of mental health. In recent years, professionals from across the varied mental health disciplines—psychiatrists, clinical psychologists, social workers, counselors, marriage and family therapists, and others—have begun to ask questions about some of the basic assumptions that form the very foundation of our work. At the heart of these questions is a growing doubt about the official diagnostic systems for mental disorder.*

This is not to say that diagnoses are meaningless. Within the healthcare system, particularly in the United States, receiving a diagnosis is critical to accessing the necessary medical care. It can also provide comfort and validation to folks who may have been dismissed in their struggles, an acknowledgment that their struggles are real. What we are challenging here is the system itself so that we can look for alternative frameworks to provide a better level of care and treatment and, ultimately, build better relationships through a more compassionate and inclusive lens.

So, how can neurotypical people who want to work with neurodivergent populations support this shift in perspective? We can start by listening to how neurodivergent people experience the world without positioning neurotypical behavior as "normal." Instead, we can embrace neurodivergent experiences and behaviors as creating a broader framework and understanding of what it is to be human, rather than positioning these experiences and behaviors as symptoms of a disorder.

Many of our students at The HERD Institute are diagnosed as neurodivergent, and many more are probably neurodivergent without an official diagnosis. We take pride in offering an inclusive environment

---

[5] Kamens S. R., Elkins D. N., & Robbins B. D. (2017). Open letter to the DSM-5. *Journal of Humanistic Psychology, 57*, 675–687. https://doi.org/10.1177/0022167817698261

that supports everyone's learning differences and ways of being in the world. The feedback that we've received points to how seldom students have felt accepted authentically in a learning environment without the need to mask their neurodivergent behaviors. This type of feedback reminds me that learning can only happen when our nervous systems are settled and regulated. Of course, this is true for all beings, human and non-human animals who have experienced trauma, but particularly for those who have adverse childhood experiences and/or belong to marginalized populations.

In a recent discussion with my dear friend, Dr. Jason Dias, author of *Values of Pain,*[6] I was sharing my frustration of how the DSM-5 has medicalized human experiences, assigning mental disorder to all but a small sliver of human generalizations that are deemed the norm. From this framework, adopting the definition that neurodivergence refers to the infinite ways of human functioning, perhaps, I mused, it means that all who are constrained by society's expectations of what "normal" and neurotypical means, are essentially living within *The Matrix*[7], constrained by the fear of being disordered as laid out in the DSM-5; forced to adhere to the strict rules and expectations of the neurotypical mind. Thus, those who have embraced their neurodivergence are the ones who have gained freedom from the broken system. Perhaps the DSM-5 is Agent Smith. I joked that maybe Jason, who identifies as autistic, was Morpheus, leading the revolution. Jason, in his infinite wisdom, identified with the cat in the movie that alerted everyone that there was a glitch in the system. This made complete sense to me, returning full circle to my question: is it the human that is disordered, or is it the system that we exist within?

Being BRAVER
Breathe. Reflect. Accept. Vulnerable. Engage. Reflect.
What are you experiencing right now? If you identify as neurodivergent, what has this brought up for you? If you identify as neurotypical, how different is this perspective for you? What are you curious about? What do you want to engage with? What are you taking from this experience?

---

[6] Dias, J. (2017). *Values of pain.* Superluminal Velocity Books.
[7] 1999 movie that posits what we think is real is simply a simulation guided by pre-determined programming.

Chapter 18

Systems of Power and Oppression

Power and oppression over others exist in all societies. I was watching *The Last of Us,* a show on Netflix about a post-pandemic world that has been infested with cordyceps that take over the human brain and turn humans into zombie-like creatures. It's a rather formulaic post-apocalyptic and dystopian trope where human beings in a fallen civilization revert to non-human animal-like behaviors. These stories often also perpetuate the belief that humans are more evolved than all other animals, superior in their intelligence, and the innate rulers of the planet we share with all other living beings. It intrigues me that this is the assumption and premise for so many of these stories, where power structures that define species, class, race, gender, and sexuality prevail despite the fall of systems and institutions as we know them. It suggests a fundamental belief that society can only function with oppressive structures in place; that this is the natural order of things, so much so that even in the creation and re-envisioning of a whole new world, we cannot bear to step away from them. Barbara Gurr's edited volume, *Race, Gender, and Sexuality in Post-Apocalyptic TV and Film* (yes, I went down that rabbit hole!), offers an in-depth analysis of this phenomenon.[1] If you've made it this far through the book, you're probably becoming familiar with the types of existential musings that occupy my thoughts.

I'm fascinated by why people believe what they believe, how they arrived at these beliefs, and how open they are to challenging them. I also hold deep curiosity for why some people feel called to challenge systemic injustice while others appear apathetic or resistant to change. In all these post-apocalyptic stories, there is a minority calling for revolution and resistance to re-establishing the status quo. Oftentimes, the rebels fighting for a revolution will win the battle, signaling hope

---

[1] Gurr, B. (2015). Introduction: After the world ends, again. In B. Gurr (Ed.), *Race, gender, and sexuality in post-apocalyptic TV and film.* Palgrave Macmillan. https://doi.org/10.1007/978-1-137-49331-6_1

and potentiality in humanity while simultaneously reinforcing that this can exist in fantasy only.

All of which leads me to more questions: What does this have to do with the equine-facilitated industry? Why is this important in our work with horses? What can we learn from our relationships with horses that will allow us to cultivate more empathy for human healing?

Parallels

Power properly understood is nothing but the ability to achieve purpose. It is the strength required to bring about social, political, and economic change.
~ Martin Luther King Jr.

Power is often understood as the ability to influence the behavior or actions of others. But for what purpose? Power is a relational concept, and while it isn't inherently positive or negative, power can be exercised in oppressive ways. Brené Brown talks about the difference between having power over another, which is often driven by fear, versus those who "share power with, empower people to, and inspire people to develop power within."[2] A "power over" mindset believes in scarcity: that power is finite and needs to be held onto tightly. This can lead to the use of force, coercion, or manipulation to control others. A power with/to/within mindset believes that power is infinite and that power is expansive. This type of power can "offer people experiencing fear and uncertainty transparency and create learning cultures based on critical thinking and evidence-based data from multiple perspectives."[3] That's the type of power I want us all to subscribe to because the power over mindset is at the core of systemic oppression.

A power over mindset means that power and oppression become two sides of the same coin. Each side exists in correlation with and because of the other. The desire to have power over another creates the desire to keep them oppressed. The subjugation of the other elevates the power-over dynamic. This continuous feedback loop results in

---

[2] Brown, B. (2018). Dare to lead: Brave work. Tough conversations. Whole hearts. Random House Publishing Group.

[3] Brown, B. (2023) *Brené Brown on power and leadership.* Retrieved from https://brenebrown.com/resources/brene-brown-on-power-and-leadership/#:~:text=Power%20over%20is%20driven%20by,people%20to%20develop%20power%20within.

oppression becoming the systematic and institutionalized use of power to subjugate and exploit a group or individual. While these dynamics are often discussed in the context of human-to-human connections, they can also be observed in the intricate bond between humans and horses. By delving into the parallels between power and oppression in human interactions and the complex relationships that humans share with horses, we can shed light on the shared patterns of dominance, control, and liberation that exist in both realms.

In human societies, this power-over dynamic can manifest itself in various forms, ranging from socioeconomic privileges, political structures, physical and economic resources, to individual and relational dynamics. In horse–human relationships, these power dynamics are inherent in our removal and limitation of freedom, choice, and agency for our horses. Our anthropomorphic lens leads us to impose our will and power over our horses; we decide how they live, who they live with, what and how often they eat, and give them jobs and expect them to perform to set expectations. We've exerted dominance over horses through dubious training techniques, incorporating harsher methods to break their will. A well-behaved horse is deemed to be "broke," but many don't question what has been broken. Can't control your horse? Here, have a harsher bit. Horse won't move? Give him a flick of the whip. Thinking back to my experience with Peter Blue, the poor riding-school pony, I remember being told the common adage of "you can't let them win," which continues to hold ground to this day in many horse training circles. The human concept of control is entwined with our flawed assumption that leadership is hierarchical and that the epitome of winning is to have power over another.

The role of the noble steed has changed significantly since the Western industrial revolution, moving from being means of transport, agricultural machines, and war heroes to providing human entertainment. These days, they are usually bought and sold as commodities and fall under the designation of livestock. Once purchased, they are put to use in a variety of settings and disciplines, from racehorse to dressage arena, and ranch horse to barrel racing, as well as partners in therapeutic programs. The general expectation is that they will be worth the price tag they came with to assist in the pursuit of medals and buckles, and to meet the needs of their human owners. This is de rigueur within this equine industry that we all belong to. These common practices are so woven into the fabric of our understanding of what it means to co-exist with horses that we rarely stop to question any of it. But if we want to shift the dynamics of power from a power-over to a power-with/to/within mindset, then we need to critically assess what our industry foundations are built from. As Nahshon Cook, horseman, poet, and author of *Horses See Us As We Are,* says so beautifully,

> For me, the beginning of a relationship with the ones in need of healing from humans happens when I accept their ability to choose freely whether or not they're willing to lead me through repairing pottery with silver or gold lacquer. Like the process of mending wounds we've inflicted using our desire for connection as code for a need to control.[4]

Historically, the domestication of animals has been hailed as co-evolution of humans and non-human animals, lauded as partnerships between man and beast, providing mutual benefit to both: wolves that became dogs and wild horses that became war heroes. Romanticizing the process of domestication frees us from the reality that the majority of our relationships with non-human animals are far from mutually beneficial. James Serpell, author of *In the Company of Animals,* asserts that domestication meant that humans became "the lord and master, the animals his servants and slaves."[5] David A. Nibert, author of *Animal Oppression and Human Violence,* goes further to declare that contrary to popular belief that the domestication of animals was beneficial to humankind, it has in fact "undermined the development of a just and peaceful world" and that "the harms that humans have done to other animals... have been a precondition for and have engendered large-scale violence against and injury to devalued humans, particularly Indigenous people around the world."[6]

Take a moment to digest that.

Nibert's thesis centers on the inevitable dehumanization of humans as a continuation of our Orwellian outlook that "all animals are created equal, but some are more equal than others." While this tangent may feel like an unnecessary truth bomb, it is highly relevant to how we bring ourselves into the work that we do as equine- facilitated practitioners. We need to understand the foundations upon which we stand and empower ourselves to change the way that we interact with

---

[4] Cook, N. (2022). *Horses see us as we are.* Nova's Books.

[5] Serpell, J. (1996). *In the company of animals: A study of human-animal relationships.* Cambridge University Press.

[6] Nibert, D. A. (2013). *Animal oppression and human violence: Domesecration, capitalism, and global conflict.* Columbia University Press.

our equine partners. Ultimately, this places all domesticated horses under the power and oppression of the humans that they belong to. Even in the language, we can begin to see and feel the power differentials in the relationships. What does it mean to *own* another sentient being? What does it mean to expect them to work for us because we own them? How do prevailing beliefs rooted in dominance theory impact the way we work with horses? What are the implications of maintaining the commodification of horses within the context of equine-facilitated work? What parallels can we draw from the way we treat our horses and all other non-human animals to the way we treat humans? Most important, how can we do things differently?

Dr. Gala Argent is a trans-disciplinary scholar of human–equine relationships and co-editor of *The Relational Horse,* a collection of essays that ask: How are human–equine relationships communicated, enacted, understood, encouraged, and restricted?[7] Argent focuses on the "who" of the horse to move away from its objectification and bring our awareness to what we refer to at The HERD Institute as an *I–Thou* way of relating. Through our conversations, I have come to appreciate the importance of understanding ethological, anthropological, and sociological perspectives in my interactions with horses. Argent emphasizes the need to center our relationships with horses as "the bidirectional, mutually influential, interactive context-driven process through which humans and horses engage together to co-create, share, and replicate overlapping identities, realities, and worlds." In this way, we can create more equine-centered practices that take into account that our horses live in captivity with degrees of suppressed autonomy.

As Nibert states, the relationship between animal oppression and human violence is intricate and multifaceted, encompassing historical, psychological, ethical, and environmental dimensions. By understanding this connection, we can address the root causes of violence and oppression, promoting a more compassionate and just society.[8] Advocating for animal rights, incorporating animal ethics into our moral frameworks, and adopting sustainable practices are essential steps toward breaking the cycle of violence. Just as there have been struggles for liberation among oppressed human groups, efforts have

---

[7] Argent G. & Vaught J. (2022). *The relational horse : How frameworks of communication care politics and power reveal and conceal equine selves.* BRILL.
[8] Nibert, D. A. (2013). *Animal oppression and human violence: Domesecration, capitalism, and global conflict.* Columbia University Press.

also been made to liberate horses from oppressive treatment. The emergence of ethical horsemanship, natural training methods, and the promotion of horse welfare serve as parallel movements to those advocating for social justice and equality among humans. These endeavors aim to empower horses, providing them with choices, respect, and better living conditions, mirroring the fight for liberation of marginalized folks in our communities. By acknowledging the intrinsic value of all sentient beings, we can pave the way for a future where animals are treated with compassion, and human violence is diminished. It is through collective efforts that we can strive for a harmonious coexistence, where both humans and animals can thrive in a world devoid of oppression and violence.

Being BRAVER

Breathe. Reflect. Accept. Vulnerable. Engage. Reflect.

Part III

Belonging in the HERD

Chapter 19

New Beginnings: Taking the First Step

I've lived in many places throughout my life—different countries, cities, and towns. Each time I move, I learn something about the way I orient myself to find my feet, to ground myself through the grief of leaving and the uncertainty of new beginnings. Some moves are more painful than others. In 2013, after a wonderful two years in Northern Virginia working as an equine-facilitated therapist specializing in eating disorders, I had to close my practice and pass it over to a trusted colleague and start again in a different state. Being told by well-meaning friends and family that "When one door closes, another one opens," left me feeling unsupported in my need to grieve. It was a new beginning that was also a painful ending.

I missed my friends and colleagues, and the herd of horses I worked with. I missed the community that I had become a part of. I missed the diversity of Northern Virginia, and I missed the woodlands where I walked with my dog. I noticed that as I tried to settle into my new life, I compared everything with what had been lost. While I was excited to begin a new journey in Ohio, I also recognized that I wasn't ready to let go and step forward wholeheartedly into it.

I was fortunate enough to be able to bring my mare, Reba, with me to Ohio, so I was able to watch her transition into her new life as I eased myself into mine. Since then, she has moved several more times to different barns before I was finally able to have my own facility and bring her home. I learned a lot from observing how she interacted with her new herds, and subsequently have been able to translate that into my own process.

Like us, horses remember their "friends," their pasture mates and caretakers, so I'm intrigued by how they deal with herd transitions and/or how they enter into a new herd. As mentioned previously, horses typically don't have a choice as to where they live or with whom they share their lives, and I'm mindful of what that's like for them.

Watching Reba meeting and greeting a new herd is fascinating to me. I am in awe of what I perceive as her ability to get her bearings of where she has arrived with such ease. Entering the herd, she is inevitably greeted by other members in turn, during which she will perform her little ritual of sniff, stamp, and squeal. I have yet to see her meet another horse without this little dance of announcing her arrival. I see it as her willingness to engage with others while setting clear boundaries right from the start. Once the dance is over, Reba always chooses to spend time by herself away from the rest of her new herd. Regardless of whether it is a large herd or a small one, a mixed herd or mares only, she will take herself away from the others to graze by herself for a while. If another horse approaches her, she will greet them cautiously and wait to see if they are demanding anything of her. If not, she will return to grazing and allow them into her space. If the other horse is approaching to claim their own space, she will move aside and find another spot for herself. In this way, within a day or so, Reba will find a pasture mate or two to graze alongside. These will become the horses that she stays loyal to during her time in that herd. They will be the ones that she greets vocally when they return to the paddock after being ridden by their owners, and they will be the ones she calls to when she walks by their stalls when I lead her through the barn.

Watching Reba, I became more aware of my own need to allow myself to take some time in surveying my new surroundings and to assess with whom I wanted to spend time with. I recognized that I needed to find my own human "herd" in order to feel connected with where I had landed and acknowledged that taking the first step toward that was not easy. It requires taking a risk to show our vulnerabilities and willingness to be open to new relationships. We are wired for connection and belonging. When we are removed from the safety of our "herd," our brains are literally searching to replace that which was lost. Stepping into a new space is anxiety provoking for many, and we deal with that anxiety in many ways: overcompensate by being extra gregarious, shrink and retreat into the safety of ourselves, or take tentative steps forward and back until we feel secure enough to reveal more of ourselves to those around us.

I don't know if Reba misses her old pasture mates from previous barns, but I do know that she is deeply attached to her current herd mates, Cheyenne and Arrow, and will call for them when they are out of sight. My three horses have been together as a herd since I moved to my own facility in 2016. Since I don't have stalls and operate an open barn environment where they can come and go as needed, they are rarely separated and almost never leave the property, and when they do travel, they travel together. While this has created what traditional horse people term "herd-bound behavior" or "barn sourness" in them, I see it as natural behavior of animals who are deeply connected. Instead of training them to desensitize their need for connection, I work with them to co-regulate by adapting to their need to be in sight of one another. On the odd occasion that I ride one of them, I make sure that the other two are in the pasture next to us. When we move from one pasture to another, instead of haltering and leading them one by one, I intentionally designed the facility to allow them to walk together from one space to another.

I am mesmerized by my herd. I could watch them all day long just going about their daily lives. There's a rhythm to their movements as they come together and give space when needed. In and out. Sometimes closer, sometimes apart. Like the filling of lungs with a deep breath in connection and the gentle exhalation and relief of being seen. The beauty of being with horses is that they help us call attention to where we are in our process. Reba has taught me with every relocation that it is imperative to remain authentic in what we are searching for: connection with others who allow us to be ourselves. It's the type of connection that is felt on an embodied level as the gradual easing of physical tension, as an opening outward to receive the beauty of friendship. It is the feeling of embracing all of oneself that may often be kept small in everyday life. It is the sensation of not needing to hide, and instead breathing in and being however we are in each moment, knowing that we will be granted deep affective reciprocity. It is the feeling of coming home to a place where one wants to linger and stay awhile.

This is the feeling that we have intentionally cultivated for our HERD community. In our post-training evaluations, our students consistently comment on the transformative impact of our culture of inclusion that allows for the ebbs and flows of connection. Regardless of who you are, where you're from, what you bring, and what you need, we are committed to holding space for connection—not through seeking but through grace—while it is available. It is not an expectation. We can lead a horse to water, but we cannot make it drink, but knowing where the water is and that there is an abundance of it, allows for a settled knowing. In this way, we become the water for each member of our herd by saying "I am here when you need me."

Chapter 20

Contemplations on the Influence of Coloniality

by Dr. Kelsey Dayle John

Can you take these moments and make them into a lifetime? When I exist in choreographed relation with my dogs and horses, I understand myself a little bit better. I run with my dogs through the valleys and canyons covering southern Arizona. A slight stream runs through us. River is water is life is movement. In this chapter, I reflect on the tension of being a Native horse woman. I am both influenced by tradition and affected by colonialism. This chapter borrows the structure of a stream: slow, weaving, winding, and steadily pooling in moments and working through them. Using movement, friction, and softness to try and better understand my relationship to horses as a Navajo woman.

I wonder about my seven-year-old self. Playful, always talking to animals. Listening and responding as if nothing was weird about this dialogue. This was my *self* before colonialism disembodied me. I was always captivated by the ways the plants merged and met one another in the ground. As a descendent of Indian boarding school survivors, I am sincerely skeptical about practices of education/schooling in both formal and informal arenas. I have identified the constraints of coloniality within every form of education, inside and outside of formal institutions. In fact, Native scholars have argued that assimilation tactics are employed in the creation of agricultural programs and outreach in the community around areas like farming, livestock care, and agricultural fairs. These are the complexities Native folks are always sorting through. I know that colonialism has affected our relationship to our animal beings.[1]

---

[1] John, Kelsey Dayle (2020). Essay: Fences tell a story of land changes on the Navajo Nation, *Edge Effects*.

Sacredness

I don't like to talk much about "traditional Navajo horsemanship" because non-Native ears perk up. They are ready to take something that belongs to our community, something that is sacred. Sacred knowledge is sacred because of its context and its specificity. Standing Rock Sioux scholar Vine Deloria argues that indigenous knowledges were never meant to be spread and generalized across the globe but are powerful because of their placed-based relevancy.[2]

Anti-racist work is sacred, too. The undoing of the doing that binds us. I've found this is the beauty of horse–human relationships and find that humans can connect through our love and respect for these beings, even if we come from different backgrounds. At an equine- facilitated learning workshop, I become seven years old again, bouncing and squealing because the horses are so cute and perfect. So, I tell them, over and over, "you are so cute and perfect, cute and perfect."

Before school, and before all the degrees, I used to just hang out with horses. I grew up in the country in Oklahoma with horses, dogs, and cats. I was never scared of horses, nor was I concerned with their performance. I just hung out with them. I was raised with the beautiful gift of watching horses "just be horses." My family was adamant about providing the most natural setting for our horses. They were on pasture year-round, and we always had a herd that socialized and created their own dynamics.

Colonization makes and sustains systems where humans and animals are forced to perform and achieve. I've spent over 25 years of my life in systems of schooling and studied the violence of the system I am embedded in. Schooling has historically been violent for Native folks and my family. Yet, we have excelled in these spaces. The complexity is ever present. I liken this to my relationship with horses in colonial systems. It is hard to make sense of the knowledge taught and learned from popular practices of horsemanship. I find that I judge myself as harshly as I judge my little mustang girl. But she pushes back on it, and listening to her helps me decolonize myself.

Horses and Indigenous Humans

Is it true that horses were colonized and domesticated? They have been used against indigenous persons and folks of color, weaponized,

---

[2] Deloria Jr, Vine (2023). *God is red: A native view of religion*. Fulcrum Publishing.

genetically modified, exploited, and enslaved. Indigenous folks and horses share so much; we have both been enslaved and domesticated.[3] We have been confined to spaces and imprisoned, assimilated.

Academia has theorized and imagined so many kinds of decolonized spaces, but academics don't generally get the space to create those relationships. Equine-facilitated learning is complex, but also simple: be with horses and humans in authentic relationship. Focus on the relationship: "It's not about the activity."[4]

Bambi and I in the Corral

One morning, I look out and Bambi is standing at the corral gate looking into the pasture. It's not huge, maybe 2.5 acres, but it's lush and hilly with enough space to sprint and stand in comfortable proximity to the three paints next door. She looks off over the gate with an expectant posture. I almost start crying because I get it. I wasn't made to be confined either; training myself is like training my mustang girl to perform in ways that are meaningless to her.

Sometimes I feel stuck with Bambi and other times I feel free. I wonder if other people feel this tension, too. I identify this tension with my internal conflict as a Native person in a white world. I've written elsewhere that colonization is essentially a set of separations that are felt most deeply by Black, Indigenous and people of color.[5] I am deeply cognizant of and concerned about the way that we impart and decorate our human-arranged social systems on the bodies of animal beings.

Decolonizing Self and System

The hardest part of the decolonial process is decolonizing yourself: Doing the work to understand the systems you are implicated in and to swim upstream to do it differently. To create relations and sustain those relations in systems of separations. Saying the thing, taking the risk, naming the racism, and letting go of the anger. Because Native folks, we have a lot to be angry about.

---

[3] Résendez, Andrés (2016). *The other slavery: The uncovered story of Indian enslavement in America*. Houghton Mifflin Harcourt.

[4] Lac, Veronica (2020). *It's not about the activity: Thinking outside the toolbox in equine-facilitated psychotherapy and learning*. University Professors Press.

[5] John, Kelsey Dayle, and Brown, Kimberly Williams (2019). Settler/colonial violences: Black and Indigenous coalition possibilities through intergroup dialogue methodology. *American Indian Culture and Research Journal, 43*(2): 135–156.

Has Colonization Affected My Relationship to Horses?

When I ask myself this question, I understand that it has affected me and my relationship with horses. Let me zoom in and out with you. We're talking about something structural, but it's deeply personal and interpersonal. One of the biggest hurdles for me is imagining myself as a horse woman. Horse people are imagined to be white male cowboy types. Not that white male cowboys are bad. I'm related to a few of those. I'm half white after all, so who better to grapple with coloniality's implications than myself?

For me, it happened when I met a mustang named Bambi at a moment when I still believed that "men break horses." Patriarchy really had me believing that "feminized"[6] qualities are ineffective for horse relationships. When I met Bambi, I was aware of schooling practices and how they normalize violence. I started to compare training methods and noticed that many conventionally accepted methods are unregulated, patriarchal, and abusive.[7]

There is a text I love titled *Weaving an Otherwise: In-Relations Methodological Practice* that describes the process of knowing and being with one another. In the final chapter, the authors offer a set of questions for research, but I ask myself these in relation to beings. One in particular: "What is the next, most responsible thing you can do to go deeper in this work?"[8] I interpret this question to be for me, my work, and my relationship with horses. Sometimes this looks like adopting a rescue horse, moving somewhere with pasture, giving her a break from training, finding her a friend, taking an equine class, listening to her body language, accommodating her feeding preferences, or finding the right professionals.

For me, systems of inequality are intimately related between human and animal.[9] Just as my people have been colonized by schooling— essentially trained to disconnect from our animal relatives. I understand I am personally affected and responsible at the same time.

---

[6] I put feminized in quotation marks because what is feminine really? Gender scholars explain that masculine and feminine are gendered social construction and that, of course, gender and sex are different categories.

[7] Also important to this learning was a class I took with Dr. Nina Ekholm Fry, who teaches equine behavior as a way to demystify training and advocate for science-based methods.

[8] Tachine, A., Nicolazzo, Z., Patel, L., & Yang, K. W. (2022). *Weaving an otherwise: In-relations methodological practice.* Stylus.

[9] Three people helped me understand this: my horse, Billy Ray Belcourt, and Zakiyah Iman Jackson.

With horses, we can't claim we have no power because simply being human is our proximity to power.

The Diné ways of knowing remind me of a time before these systems, and even moments in the now. It is beautiful because she is beautiful. Everything about her is good.

Everything about Łį́į́' is Good[10]

When I close my eyes in dark places
   I see parallel sand lines of red mesascapes
     and that's my escape
When I'm in silent places
  and my tongue can't signal sounds for how I feel
     I think about the materials that made me
   carrying up and down breaths of spirit and sound

When I'm all alone
   I take myself back to the place
    I'm no longer alone
I was never alone

When all the world seems violent
   I look out to shílį́į́'[11]
     And realize everything about her is good
Everything about her is good.

---

[10] This poem was originally published as the ending few lines of my dissertation. I think I remember a line from the documentary *Horse Tribe*, which chronicles a Diné horse trainer's journey working with Nez Perce horses and youth, in which Rudy Shebala says, "everything about a horse is good."

[11] I use the Navajo translation of "my horse" here because shiłį́į́' is different translationally than the English connotation of "my" as possession of the horse. It's about partnership with the horse and relationship through the Diné clan system.

Chapter 21

My Misfit Tomboy Life with Horses

by Yoshi Babcock

The emancipation of women may have begun not with the vote, nor in the cities where women marched and carried signs and protested, but rather when they mounted a good cow horse and realized how different and fine the view. From the back of a horse, the world looked wider.
~ Joyce Gibson Roach[1]

I was born in Japan in the late 1970s, and it is fair to say I was a tomboy who did not fit into my generation's conventional Japanese female role. Throughout my childhood, my favorite thing to do was to ride a bike and explore the neighborhood. I do not recall playing with dolls, but can clearly remember catching bugs and fish, mostly with boys. Also, being skinny and tan, people often thought that I was a boy, which led my mother to take me to a beauty parlor to get my hair permed, hoping that I would look more feminine. She also had me wear sundresses and skirts, but they ended up torn most of the time.

So how did this misfit tomboy from a small city in Japan first encounter a horse? My very first memory of riding a horse was when my family took a summer vacation in Nagano when I was in elementary school. Nagano is in the central part of the main island of Japan (*Honshu*), which has many beautiful mountains and natural landscapes. It is also home to Kiso horses, which are one of eight indigenous horse breeds native to Japan. I remember a farmer offering rides by leading a horse around a large round pen for 500 yen (approximately $5 US). When I saw that, I had this strong urge to ride the horse, so I did! Once again, not typical behavior for a Japanese girl, but it is what my heart longed for in that moment.

My misfit tomboy life continued throughout middle school and high

---

[1] Roach, J. G. (1990). *The cowgirls.* University of North Texas Press.

school. I was an academically strong student but hung out with students who were labeled "troublemakers." As a result, I got bullied, and my life was literally turned upside down, negatively affecting my academic career and mental health. By the time I reached high school, I began failing most of my classes, except for having perfect grades in English. One day, my homeroom teacher approached me and asked if I would be interested in applying for a scholarship to become an exchange student in the United States. Like the time I had a strong urge to hop on a Kiso horse, I had a strong desire to apply, leading to another profound moment in my life that changed me forever. I ended up winning the scholarship and was gifted the opportunity to stay in Oregon for one summer. One of my fondest memories from that time was also riding a horse, but this time on the beach. I remember my host mother reminding me that Japan is on the other side of the Pacific Ocean, where the sun sets on that beach. That was the moment I learned how big the world was and how proud I felt of myself for traveling so far!

Growing up by the sea, the beach became one of my favorite places, whether I am in Japan or elsewhere in the world. Riding horses in the wide-open space with the huge body of water made it extra special. I do not recall having any fears, just a desire to keep going. Counter to the conformity ingrained in me through my Japanese upbringing, I found myself separating from the rest of the group and riding out on my own. This was probably the first moment I experienced being wild and free. It was a true reflection of my 17-year-old self's curiosity and longing for independence and one of the most profound moments: I felt my true self aligned with the essence of the moment that this horse gifted me.

After completing the exchange program, I wanted very much to study more in the US and decided to transfer schools. Don't ask me how I knew that was the right thing to do at that time, but I knew it with the whole of my being. Looking back, it almost seems insane, but I'm glad I made the decision in my senior year of high school to transfer to a boarding school in upstate New York, and subsequently to Michigan for college and graduate school. I cannot thank my parents enough for supporting me, and I recognize the privilege of being able to follow my heart in this way.

Once again, my misfit tomboy life continued, now into my adulthood. After completing my master's degree in clinical psychology, I ended up taking a temporary position as a Japanese/English interpreter at an automotive company; that's where I ended up meeting my husband. He is white and was born and raised in a "sundown city" in Michigan where there was a clear division between Black and White folks in the 1960s and 1970s. Unfortunately, some of his family members did not welcome me because of my race, religious upbringing, and immigration status. Oh well, I already had experience being a misfit, right?

In the summer of 2010, I took a job as a research assistant at a medical school as a bilingual clinical psychologist in Sendai (northern city in Honshu). While working there, the Great East Earthquake and Tsunami hit in March of 2011, and I had to make an emergency return to Michigan. I survived, but the experience forced me to do some serious soul-searching, and that's when horses showed up in my life once again.

After returning from Japan, I returned to a 9-to-5 corporate job as an interpreter because I was not ready to work as a psychologist. After experiencing an unexpected, life-altering event like the earthquake and tsunami, I was experiencing acute symptoms of PTSD and needed to do something about it. I kept searching, and an interesting thing happened in the fall of 2016 while my husband and I took a vacation to Granbury, Texas. While we were there, we visited the Fort Worth Stockyards to watch the barrel races. We were both mesmerized by the striking presence of the horses. My husband kept saying "horses are majestic," and meanwhile, I felt like lightning had struck me. The next thing I knew, I had tears rolling down my cheeks. I felt waves of joy and excitement surging through me, sweeping away my awareness of everything else. It was so visceral that I felt my body shaking and I knew something inside me, something integral to who I am, had permanently changed in the same way that the earthquake and tsunami in Japan had changed my life forever. I wasn't going to walk away from this as the same person I had been. At that moment, when I witnessed these beautiful animals and their uncompromising power, I was determined to find a way to work with them. I felt that I had finally found a piece of my life that I wasn't even aware was missing. As strong waves of emotions coursed through me, I was reminded of a similar feeling: that moment when I knew I had to come to the US to study.

Shortly after returning from my trip, I met a friend from work who serendipitously mentioned that he was thinking of taking horseback riding lessons at a local barn. Overflowing with the inspiration from my recent embodied realization, I quickly signed up for lessons, too. My husband was so intrigued by my joy and energy when it came to horses that he decided that he wanted to pursue them with me. Once he started, there was no going back for him either. The magnetic lure of the horses had ensnared him as well. Soon our lives began revolving around horses. First, we signed up for other riding lessons at local barns and became well known as this weird, inter-racial couple who loved to groom and hand graze horses. Next, we volunteered at a rescue farm to gain more experience. Eventually, my misfit tomboy nature nudged me to seek healing work with horses, and I became certified as an equine-guided learning coach while also returning to work as a psychologist. Currently, I work in private practice, bringing my passion for horses into equine-facilitated psychotherapy sessions. It was during this transition to private practice that I found The HERD Institute.

I met Veronica for the first time in person at an Inclusive HERD™ workshop in Ohio. This prompted me to attend a HERD equine-facilitated psychotherapy practicum to get a better feel for the certification program. Honestly, I was wary at first. I was worried about entering an existential–humanistic based learning space again as I had lost faith in humanistic psychology after completing my graduate program. My experiences as a racial minority and non-native speaker at the school felt extremely isolating, and I did not want to relive the experience. But my experience at the HERD practicum gave me the chance to make peace with my graduate school wound. To be honest, I was shocked to experience such a safe space to learn as a racial minority because I had given up searching for such a place. As I immersed myself further in the program, I realized how much I missed the existential–humanistic approach. I again fell in love with this way of working—this time with horses. What a bonus!

I believe I have undergone a transformation as part of this training experience, complete with a "phoenix rising" moment at my last practicum. Finally, after a long incubation period, I came out of the ashes and started stretching my wings. I am beginning to embrace my essence as Yoshi. I feel centered and settled, gentle yet strong. The inclusive, accepting, and safe training space provided the opportunity to make peace with my graduate school wound and allowed me to move forward with myself being me, which includes embracing my Japanese lineage. I had a chance to embody self-acceptance and share my authentic self with other participants, who were mostly white and representative of a space I would previously not have felt safe enough to share in. I recognized that it was time for me to stop rewriting my story and begin writing a new chapter. I witnessed that a sense of belongingness can promote enormous healing, helping to build self-confidence. Now, I feel it is time for me to step into my power.

When I entered the horse world, which I have experienced as such a white space, I was fearful of facing racial discrimination. And I have experienced some discomforting moments. People were not accustomed to seeing an Asian woman with a white husband floating around in the barn, and they simply did not feel comfortable. However, despite our discomfort, I kept going because of my passion for horses. My experience with the HERD training has helped me to access my internal resources, which includes my Japanese lineage. I felt like I broke up with Japan when I left as a teenager, but as I reclaimed this part of me, I started seeing Japan through the lens of horses and realized that there is so much wisdom in ancient Japanese culture that I appreciate. I also started seeing more of a panoramic view of life rather than only focusing on specifics. Maybe it is because I'm starting to operate from a place of ease rather than urgency. I feel that I have space to breathe and respond now. I'm finally accessing my essence without feeling concerned for my safety. Maybe this is what confidence feels like in my body—feeling safe in my own body and letting my brilliance shine through. I also feel full but empty at the same time. It feels like everything but nothing all at once. Maybe that's what *being* feels like?

Who knew that the skinny, tan, misfit tomboy from a small city in Japan would end up in Michigan to do healing work with horses? Looking back, I am so glad I always followed my heart and intuition and that I continue to do so. I am also grateful that my dear husband genuinely enjoys connecting with horses as I do, and we get to share these experiences together. Although we do not own horses, we keep encountering people who graciously offer to ride with us and let us partner with their horses for my healing work. I strive to offer the type of inclusive space that I have experienced within the HERD and with horses to support others in finding their authentic expressions of themselves.

My life has been quite unconventional. My skin continues to be tan and my hair straight and short. My dear mother, who lives in Japan, still advises me to perm my hair and avoid letting myself become any tanner. It makes me chuckle because like the quote from Joyce Gibson Roach, my view of life is so much wider now that horses have come into my life, and there is no going back.

Chapter 22

Allyship

by Catherine Manakas

I'm a white straight cisgender woman. And sometimes I am an ally of Black, Indigenous, and People of Color. There are times I don't get it right. In my early college days, I began to understand my own struggles as a woman living in a patriarchal society. I learned about power structures and became aware of how ingrained these ways of thinking are for most people. Later in college I met my friend Brian, a gay man. His ongoing everyday challenges followed the same patterns as my own. Note that our problems were not the same; rather they followed the same patterns. It was logical and felt natural to become his ally. We co-led the gay rights group on our college campus.

Most of my college professors were Black women. I learned a lot from these professors and have a deep respect for them. And yet I wasn't internally committed to allyship to Black and Brown people. Not like I was to the LGBTQIA community. I could understand racism in a logical way. Power structures were similar. But something slippery inside of me avoided committing to becoming an ally.

I was raised to believe our great country is a melting pot of colors and cultures. The melting process melds us together; other cultural identities become a part of our own. We will graciously assimilate everyone. As a result, we don't have to talk about our skin color. Because we are a melting pot.

Meanwhile, instead of dissolving themselves into any melting pot, Black, Indigenous, and people of color maintain a vibrant community and culture, cultivating a sense of belonging without diluting themselves. They support one another through the everyday taxations of living within a white space. While they cultivated their connections, white people convinced one another we were all the same and that acknowledging differences was shameful. It is a hard realization to know you are part of the problem, particularly when you don't have words for any of it. Becoming an ally for racial justice means understanding something I had no words for while I was growing up— my whiteness.

To commit oneself as a white person to being a Black person's ally means accepting that my life is easier because of my skin color. Of course, my life has been hard. And it could have been harder had I been born with a different skin color. In reverse, I need to also realize that my Black or Brown friend has a more difficult life because of society's preference for my skin color. So, not only has my life been easier for my skin color, but my friend's life has been harder for her skin color.

I committed myself to becoming an ally to brown and Black people while sitting in a Red Lobster with my friend Aretha. About fifteen years ago, Aretha and I worked together as equal rights officers. We made the initial state-level probable-cause decision about whether discrimination occurred within a workplace or housing situation. We would often go to lunch together. Madison, Wisconsin is a university town and the center of state government.

Aretha talked to me about her life. We bonded over our childhood experiences. We both grew up with mothers who had mental health challenges, so we share a particular kind of trauma related to that, and I developed a fierce affection for my friend during those conversations. One day, she shared an experience with me. She described being a kid and playing at a white friend's house. The friend's brother and his friends chased Aretha into a closet yelling at her, repeating what they deemed to be Black names, trying to guess her name. It struck me that this was something I had never experienced in my childhood, a trauma that was different than the one we shared.

About a day after she told me this story, I checked in with her, apologizing for this awful experience. Sharing something like that must have left her feeling bruised. She chuckled. Sure, it was scary at the time, but she was okay. I was stunned. How could she be okay? But she was okay. She was smiling at me with amusement in her eyes.

It dawned on me that I was more upset than she was. She had had years to process this experience with other Black people who understood the experience and gave her language to process it. *I was the one new to racism.* Her telling me this story had an impact on me. Her telling me this story was not particularly impactful for her.

But I wasn't new to racism. My friend and I worked as equal rights officers for the state. We conducted investigations and made probable-cause findings on accusations of racism. I had heard stories of racism before. I mean, I listened to the news and lived in the same world. I wasn't in a vacuum. Why did this old story of a relatively small injury impact me so deeply?

Because I was in a vacuum. Because I existed in the same world as my friend without truly connecting to race. I had understood white privilege, and colonialism and implicit bias in a theoretical way. I had been learning about those concepts since I co-led a gay rights group in college. Learning about race and living race are two different things.

During our next trip to Red Lobster, I really looked at Aretha. How her eyebrows feathered to a stop. How the curls at her temple lay against her skin. Her smile as I pushed all the biscuits toward her (because she delighted in the fact that I'm gluten intolerant). I looked her deep in the eyes and said, "It must be so exhausting. Teaching people like me." She said it was. And that sometimes it was worth it.

In the beginning of my social justice learning I gravitated to the causes that either directly affected me or that which was so like my own experiences that I needn't work terribly hard to see myself in that person's shoes. I could relate to the LGBTQIA community. My gay friend had all the same safety concerns about dating men that I had. Additionally, he was seeking a sense of community, of belonging, just like I was. And in its efforts to dismantle the discrimination it faces, the LGBTQIA community celebrates itself and encourages everyone to be self-accepting. It feels darn good to find a community of people who encourage you to accept and celebrate yourself. It was easy to be an ally of this group. Becoming an LGBTQIA ally was validating and felt good.

Becoming an ally of my Black friend evolved differently. And there are reasons for that difference. I was raised in a world that considered it a virtue to be blind to color. Acknowledging color was to acknowledge the differences in people. And the differences in people are often manufactured by culture. If you cannot see color, then you cannot see that the world treats people differently because of their color. And if you do not see how the world treats people of color differently than white people, then you cannot possibly acknowledge their everyday struggles.

My friend Aretha had a support network in place. She had family and church and friends and wasn't starved for a sense of community. Why would she need to reach out to a white person who was programmed to not acknowledge her everyday struggles? Why would she risk being vulnerable with someone like me?

Becoming an ally of my Black friend didn't feel good like being an LGBTQIA ally felt good. My friend was initially reserved. She didn't want to genuinely reach out in friendship just to be told her problems aren't problems, that she is overreacting, and otherwise be gaslit. There was very little potential benefit for her in extending friendship to me.

When we work in equine-facilitated learning sessions, our focus is on holding emotionally safe spaces, the relationship between those participating in the session and their connection to each other. When we create a safe space, we put intention into that act. I picture it as a bubble I deliberately place around us. I attempted to create a safer space for my friend in the middle of Red Lobster during a lunch rush. And while I may have done this as a loving act,so my friend felt safer with me, it set the stage for me to be just as influenced by the interaction about to occur. I realized that she was also holding a safer space for me to explore my process of becoming an ally.

By co-creating this space at our table, in which the server began to feel like an intruder, we both felt connected to each other. Connection is a fluid thing. Aretha led me to see her not as some unrelatable other like I had been taught as a child. Rather she allowed me to see how she embodies her Blackness and vitality and spark all woven together to create this amazing individual.

This moment carried with it all the weight of any other I–Thou experience. Co-creating a safer space does something else dynamic. It encourages everyone in the bubble to be present. I can't hold space if my mind is elsewhere. And I can't let my mind wander when someone holds space for me, showing that level of interest in me as a person. So, the parties involved are engaged in the moment. Even though my friend and I shared some past stories, we were focused on how that connected us. We were tending to each other in that moment. We were present in the here and now moment.

It was after the moment had passed that I had to reconcile my new understanding of reality: that Black people are treated less favorably in the same world we share because of their Blackness. A concept I'd long known and yet hadn't allowed to sink deeply into my awareness of race. She was little moved by the retelling of an old story. I was rebuilding my reality with new eyes.

The concepts that make equine-facilitated learning so profound for participants were profound in my deepening understanding of race in the United States. It was not in educating myself, though those efforts likely prepared me for the reality, but it was in connecting to one individual with whom we stayed present in the moment for each other to listen and be listened to. As equine-facilitated learning practitioners, we can encourage this type of allyship. We have the tools to encourage others to connect to those who are different and experience life differently. We can hold space for each other, stay present in the here and now, and connect.

This process is hard. Black, Indigenous, and people of color are exhausted battling the programming many of us white people still hang onto. And for white folks, understanding that we don't understand a lot of our world is unsettling. Our horses can make it less hard. Our horses don't understand institutionalized racism, but they excel at co-regulation. They excel at creating emotionally safer spaces and staying present. They will hold space when the teaching is tough. They will hold space when the learning is tough. And having their help as we teach and learn means we can do hard things with more support.

Understanding power structures and how people struggle is one piece of the puzzle of allyship. Understanding how different our lives are is an important step toward enacting change. But to recommit every morning to antiracism takes something stronger. For me that took loving my friend. Relating to someone who has had a different life while living side by side in the same society, reaching over and connecting to that person, that creates the commitment. Connection to my friend made me want to be an ally for racial justice.

However, there is one more piece to note. Calling myself an ally does not make me an ally. Both parties do not get to decide if, as a white ally, I am truly an ally. Only the person I am being an ally *to* can decide that. To be an ally in the context of equity work means more than good intentions. Would your Black, Indigenous and people of color friends and acquaintances call you an ally? Black, Indigenous and people of color individuals know when a white person isn't really in it to get their hands dirty, when a person has intentions but is unwilling to take action or make an impact. Have you ever had a friend smile and nod, then fail to help you when you really needed it? We have all been gaslit. We all know this feeling.

It wasn't until many years later, after I got an antiracism op-ed published in my conservative local newspaper in which I mention my friend Aretha, that I received my first and only invitation to the barbeque. And that was the moment I became an ally. Because she named me an ally.

There are two themes to my story of allyship. One theme is my growth process as I woke up to the reality of race. This was an internal process. The second theme is the attachment and connection I feel for a friend, that moment when I really saw her not as other but as a soul shining through her eyes. This was a relational shift in my perception. These themes intertwined and supported each other. These themes are reflected in our work as equine-facilitated learning practitioners, and I look forward to discovering more ways my horses can help support allies in the making.

Part IV

The Work of The HERD[1]

---

[1] **Please note:** Chapters 29 & 30 in this section are contributions from two HERD Institute members based in the United Kingdom. In my academic development, I have learned to write in a style that is acceptable to the American Psychological Association's standards. This required adapting to an entirely new referencing format, spelling, and grammar, and eradicating the "Britishness" of my written voice. This format is now so embedded that I no longer have to pause when I write. I have fully adopted my Americanized authorship. It occurred to me, though, that in inviting scholars to contribute to this book, the irony of "translating" and correcting spelling and sentence structures to American standards within the context of a discussion about celebrating diversity, equity, and inclusion, would be too much to bear. I want to honor the author's authentic voices in this space. To this end, I have kept the British spelling and grammar of these two chapters.

Chapter 23

Journey to Fertile Ground

I was inconsolable. Every fiber of my being ached with an emptiness that I knew would now never be filled. My muscles were sore, and my stomach and thighs were covered in bruises from injections. After eight cycles of fertility treatment, almost ten years of a grueling monthly repetition of hope and despair, my husband and I had reached the end of our journey in trying to conceive. Our final round of treatment was unsuccessful, and I was finally waving the white flag of defeat. I had cried myself dry and I was exhausted. Part of me wanted to crawl into bed and stay there, cocoon myself from the inevitable questions from family and friends who were waiting and hoping for good news, and who I knew would attempt to stay cheerful or offer reminders for me to stay strong. Another part of me wanted to scream and yell, rail against the universe for not giving me my heart's desire, and for having to fight so hard for something that came so easily for others, but still falling short. I knew that I needed to grieve, but I was afraid of the darkness that this might bring. So instead, I went to the barn and sought refuge.

Hearing the rattling of the gate, Rupert looked up from grazing. He whinnied and came cantering across the field to meet me. Stopping in front of me, he nickered softly, exhaled, shook his thick black mane, and put his head on my shoulder. I reached up and hugged him around his neck, burying my face in his mane and breathed him in. I felt myself relax some of the tension I had been holding as I immersed myself in his scent. I let go of his neck, and he positioned himself so that his belly was in front of mine. I draped my arms over him, dropping my head onto his back and melted into him. I could feel his warmth through my body, and him breathing beneath me. Matching my breath to his, I slowly let go and began to cry. Moving toward his shoulder, I leaned into his solid frame and stroked his neck. Rupert turned his head toward me and gently nudged me in my belly. Softly, he caressed me with his muzzle, moving up toward my chest and exhaled. I'm not sure how long we stood in the field like this, but I drew strength from the interaction as each minute passed. I stopped crying and took a deep breath to recenter myself. As I pulled away from Rupert, he stretched out his neck and placed his head on my shoulder and exhaled before walking back out toward his pasture mates to graze peacefully once more.

Fast forward a few years, and I found myself working with Barbara Rector and her equine specialist, Anna Calek, at her program in Tucson, Arizona. I was about to complete my doctoral program and had shared with Barbara and Anna my dreams of publishing the outcome of my research, and of creating a training institute to teach the framework that had emerged from my dissertation.

I'd chosen to work with Wild Thing, a beautiful chestnut mare, who was playful and inquisitive. She was full of energy as I led her into the arena, jogging in place as I navigated the gate, eager to be let loose. I had fully expected Wild Thing to be true to her name and take off around the arena the moment I took her halter off. To my surprise, she stayed next to me and exhaled deeply. Barbara had invited me to be with Wild Thing; however, I felt comfortable while getting to know her. I wanted to give her some space so that she could choose where she wanted to be in relation to me in the arena, so I took a few steps away. She followed. We repeated this dance for a few minutes with me changing pace and direction while she followed my every move. I was aware that while I was reveling in the playfulness of the moment, I was also feeling tension in my belly. The "game" shifted from joyfulness of being followed to curiosity about how I could get away. This, too, was a surprise. As this felt sense of needing to escape grew, Wild Thing became more persistent in what I experienced as her need for attention. No longer content with following my steps, she began to nudge my elbow and shoulder with her muzzle, and I noticed that I was backing away from her with each nudge. While I didn't feel unsafe with her, I was conscious of needing to be intentional in my movements and became intrigued by what it was she needed from me. I wondered if she needed me to move in a more purposeful direction *with her*, rather than away from her. So, I started walking the length of the arena, and Wild Thing walked with me, synchronizing her steps with mine. In spending time with horses, I'd often been invited to connect with them by intentionally matching their steps, but this was the first time that I had experienced a horse matching their steps with mine. It was a profound, powerful, and poignant moment.

As we debriefed the experience, Barbara asked me what it was I was moving away from, and what allowed me to be in sync with Wild Thing. I took a deep breath, exhaled, and began to cry. I shared my journey of infertility, my helplessness and despair, my diminished sense of worth as a woman in my inability to bring new life into the world, and how hard it was to find peace with the finality of that journey. I described the inner conflict I experienced when two years into our assessment process of becoming adoptive parents in England, my husband was offered an opportunity for us to relocate to the United States. We had intentionally let go of the adoption process, knowing that it would be too costly and complex to continue from the US. While this was a conscious choice, it was still a painful one. In my interaction with Wild Thing, I had felt a shift and became aware that setting an intention helped me to move forward with her. I knew I needed to move forward from my infertility journey but wasn't sure what that meant. Sitting beside me, Barbara gently placed her hand on my knee. Looking deep into my eyes, she said "My dear, there are so many ways to be fertile, and your fertility may not be in the human realm. Give birth to your book, your institute, and all that your being wants to bring forth into this world. Set your intention."

Fast forward a few more years, and we are about to celebrate the institute's seventh birthday. This year, I was moved to tears when a HERD member sent me a text on Mother's Day. Knowing that this day is always accompanied by grief for me, she wanted me to know that in her mind the definition of a mother is an important female figure in the origin and early history of something, and one who shapes and changes the lives of those in her care; for that reason she wanted to wish me a Happy Mother's Day on behalf of all those I have cared for as a human educator and therapist, and guardian of my non-human children. This shift in perspective feels so precious to me and allows me to hold both grief and gratitude simultaneously.

In continuing this journey, I'm reminded of the lessons that Rupert and Wild Thing have taught me. What am I moving toward and who am I journeying with? How do my values and beliefs show up in my intentionality? And how can I take care of myself and ask for support while doing all that to cultivate a more fertile ground for all?

Chapter 24

The HERD in Action

For a long while, I have wanted to share the work of our HERD community as examples of how centering diversity, equity, and inclusion in our approach to working with horses can lead to powerful transformations individually and collectively. I feel honored to witness our students' growth and learning through their training process and humbled by the impact of the work they do in their own communities. Part of my motivation in creating The HERD Institute is my belief in the power of the collective. I wanted to create more opportunities for people to access community programs that are culturally sensitive and there's only so much I can offer on my own. Plus, I figured it would be more fun to create a community of like-minded people who can help to create a tipping point for change.

A Brief Introduction to The HERD Model™[1]

HERD stands for Human-Equine Relational Development. This means that we believe in the bi-directional nature of the relationship between horses and humans, placing equal priority on the welfare of the horses as that of the people we work with. The HERD Model™ of equine-facilitated psychotherapy and learning is based on existential–humanistic and Gestalt psychology principles and holds The HERD 3 Key Principles at its foundation: The here and now; What and How; and I and Thou.

The here and now refers to our ability to remain in the present moment in a fully embodied way. This includes not only our awareness of what we are thinking, but also what we are feeling in our body through all of our senses. It also incorporates what our intuitive feelings in each moment might be. What and How refers to the process by which

---

[1] For a more in-depth discussion on The HERD Model™, please refer to Lac, V. (2020). *It's not about the activity: Thinking outside the toolbox of equine facilitated psychotherapy & learning.* University Professors Press.

the practitioner holds a sense of curiosity about what is unfolding in the relationship between the client and the horse(s), without jumping to our own interpretations, simply reflecting back our observations to our clients and allowing them to make meaning of this themselves. With regard to the welfare of our equine partners, this means paying attention to the subtlest of movements and behaviors as they interact with our clients. I and Thou refers to the philosophical concept of Martin Buber, who distinguishes between an immersive experience of being with another versus an objectified relationship. Holding an I–Thou attitude supports us to be able to become more attuned with the present moment within the relationship and acknowledge that one cannot avoid making an impact on, or being impacted by, others.

Through these 3 Key Principles, we engage with our clients in the present moment, allowing them to make meaning of the experience themselves and focus on bringing awareness to how they are interacting with us and our equine partners in the actuality of the emerging relationships. In other words, we work not only with metaphors within the therapy and learning process but also with deepening the relationships themselves.

The following chapters offer case studies and experiences of working within the HERD approach. I have included one of my own cases and am delighted to be able to share a selection of cases from our HERD faculty, graduates, and students to highlight how we can organically attend to issues of diversity, equity, and inclusion in our work with horses within a cultural competency framework. Details of the clients have been changed to protect confidentiality. These examples are not intended as a step-by-step process for practitioners to bring up issues of diversity, equity, and inclusion with the people they serve. Rather, they are offered as examples of what can emerge if we are open to exploring these issues with our clients and those in our wider community.

Chapter 25

A Different Kind of Boy

Riley was referred to me through a local non-profit that works with LGBTQIA youth. Riley identified as male and used the pronouns he/him/his and was quick to let me know that this was his chosen name. His "dead name," or the name that his parents had given him, was Helen. Riley had been using his chosen name for over a year outside of the family home, but his parents were still using his dead name. At 15 years old, Riley was a keen soccer player, and stood around 5' 8" tall with a stocky build. He lived in what he described as a very white neighborhood and felt that his presence as a 15-year-old African American boy was beginning to "freak people out." He was suffering from depression and anxiety; aside from being on the soccer team, he didn't engage in any social activities outside of school. He had also been experiencing some bullying at school since transitioning his gender identity, which had led him to isolate himself even more.

With this information, I knew that Riley was at a high risk for suicide. According to the 2020 Trevor Project survey of LGBTQIA youth in the United States, 52% of transgender and non-binary youth have seriously considered suicide. Fifty-two percent. While Riley had not yet revealed any suicidal ideation, this statistic was certainly in my awareness.

At our first session, Riley arrived at the barn with his mom. It was a cold, crisp morning in Ohio, and the overnight frost was still glistening in the early light. As Riley got out of the car, I noticed that he was wearing a plain black t-shirt with black jeans, black boots, and a grey beanie hat. I heard his mom pleading with him to take his jacket with him, which he responded to by slamming the car door and walking away. Mom got out of the car and ran after him with the black, puffy, down jacket.

> Mom: Helen! Stop being ridiculous. It's cold. Put this on!
> Riley: (Sigh) I'm fine. I don't need it.
> Mom: Just take the damn thing. Just in case.

Riley: (Sigh) I. Don't. Need. It.

His mom looked at me and threw up her hands, indicating that she'd leave the jacket hanging on the fence. I nodded and turned to Riley to welcome him into the space. He stuck his hands in his pockets and looked down at the ground as I introduced myself and went through my usual safety instructions in preparation to go into the barn. The horses were already turned out for the day in the back paddock, so I invited Riley to walk through the barn with me toward the herd.

As we walked past his jacket on the fence post, Riley reached over, picked it up, and put it on. I smiled and told him that I was glad that he was taking care of himself. "I would've just put it on if she'd called me by my name," he said. And so our work began.

We made our way through the barn and out toward the back paddock where my horses were munching on hay. Arrow, my gelding, lifted his head up and turned to watch us as we walked up to the fence line. Slowly, he began to meander his way toward us. The two mares, Reba and Cheyenne, continued to graze. Riley stepped forward as Arrow approached the gate and stretched his neck out. After sniffing Riley's shoulder, Arrow shook his head and blew out a big breath, startling himself and the boy. Riley laughed and reached his hand out to stroke Arrow's neck.

Riley: (laughing) Did I make you sneeze? You're a silly…
Riley paused. Turning to me, he asked, "Is he a boy or a girl?"
Me: Well, he's a gelding. Which means he's been neutered.
Riley: So, you still refer to him as "he"?
Me: I do. I guess that's traditional in the horse world to refer to geldings as "he."
Riley: So he's a…different…kind of boy. Kind of like me, then?

Riley smiled and continued petting Arrow on his neck. I asked him how he felt about Arrow approaching him as a fellow "different kind of boy." Riley paused his petting momentarily as he considered my question.

Riley: I guess I feel like we can be friends. But I think Arrow would like to use the pronoun "they" instead of "he."
Me: I can see how important that is to you.

> Riley: It is. It's not that difficult to make the effort and you get used to it pretty quickly. I don't know why it's so hard for people.
> Me: Well...I'd like to honor that request and I know I might slip up because I'm so used to referring to Arrow as "he." So, I'm going to do my best to transition and please feel free to correct me when I slip up. Is that okay?

Riley nodded. I asked him how he would like to get to know his new friend, and he suggested going into the paddock to be closer to Arrow. Once inside the paddock, I asked Riley to look around to take in his surroundings and notice where he wanted to position himself.

> Riley: I'd like to go and sit under the tree over there, but I also want to be close to Arrow.
> Me: How might you invite them to walk with you to the tree?
> Riley: Well, I could just throw a rope around their neck and make them come with me, but I don't want to do that. I don't know how else to make a horse do something they don't want to.
> Me: What makes you say they don't want to?
> Riley: I guess I don't know that. Do you think if I start walking over there, they'd follow me?
> Me: I don't know. How would you feel about giving it a go?

Meanwhile, Arrow had stayed by Riley's side, with a low head and eyes half closed. Riley shook his head at my question.

> Me: What's happening for you right now?
> Riley: I just know that they won't want to come with me.
> Me: I notice that they have been standing next to you since we came into the paddock. What's that like for you?
> Riley: I suppose they're happy enough to stay so that makes me feel they're with me.
> Me: What does being "with" you mean?
> Riley: I'm usually all alone, like I'm either the odd one out or just invisible. Arrow's here with me. So, I'm not alone.

I paused and allowed him to feel into that, encouraging him to reach out and feel Arrow's physical presence and to notice how Arrow responded to his touch. After a few moments of gently stroking Arrow's neck, Riley leaned in and buried his head and began to weep quietly into Arrow's mane.

> Me: I want you to really take in what it's like to be here with Arrow. To not be alone. I see your tears and I see he's turned his head toward you. How do you feel?
> Riley: They.
> Me: Yes, thank you for the correction. They've turned their head toward you. What's that like for you?
> Riley: It's like they're really looking at me.
> Me: I noticed that you took a step backward when you said tha,t and Arrow's now turned their head. What do you make of that?
> Riley: Ugh…. story of my life!

With that, Riley turned and started walking toward the willow tree in the middle of the paddock. I allowed him to lead the way, staying a few paces behind him, and watched as Arrow slowly turned and followed him. Our little procession made its way across the field: Riley, then Arrow, then me. As he approached the tree, my two mares lifted their heads, watching the procession from their vantage point on the other side of the field. They whinnied, snorted, and then dropped their heads to continue grazing. Arrow remained focused on Riley.

> Riley: They followed me!
> Me: They did. Did you hear the girls whinnying?
> Riley: Yes. But I don't think they want to join us here. They're just doing their own thing. But Arrow's here. (Turning to Arrow) I can't believe you followed me. I walked away because I thought you were done with hanging out. (Turning to me) I don't like it when people look at me. I feel like everyone's always looking at me or talking about me behind my back. Like, "Look at that freak." And now, they're talking about how I might not be allowed to play soccer with the girls, but I'm also not allowed to try out for the boys' team. My parents don't get it either. My dad keeps asking me why I'd want to "choose" to be a Black man in this world when it's hard enough to be a Black woman. Like he thinks this is optional and I'm doing it for attention. They do what the other horses are doing—tell me they care but then turn their backs. (Turning back to Arrow) But you get it, though, don't you? I mean, you didn't choose to

transition yourself; it was kinda forced on you, but you know what I mean.

Riley let out a big sigh. Arrow let out a big breath. I exhaled deeply. I found myself caught up momentarily in the parallel between human and non-human animal oppression; that through the process of neutering and spaying our animals we were inflicting our will over their natural way of being, and how this was so relevant for all the minoritized clients that I work with. I was aware that Riley's experiences of discrimination were at the intersectionality of both being Black and being transgender. I felt the heaviness of this burden upon his young shoulders and my heart ached for him. I wanted to empower him to show up and be visible in his life, but I also felt hugely protective of him, knowing that to do so meant taking enormous risks. I was in awe of the courage he showed me in this session, revealing his loneliness and isolation of not being seen, the simultaneous desire and fear of being seen, and the resulting consequences of being seen. I could hear in his statements about Arrow how important it was for him to find others like him; the importance of representation for young LGBTQIA and Black, Indigenous, and people of color; the need for mentors in our society who have gone through their own battles to help guide those behind them. Most of all, in that moment, I wanted Riley to sink into the support he was feeling from Arrow, through this strange kinship of gender reassignment.

In subsequent sessions with Riley, we returned again and again to his experiences of being seen and not seen. The choices that emerged in each session allowed him to connect to his embodied experiences of belonging and not belonging in different arenas of his life. His gender identity and transitional journey were supported by his relationship with Arrow and empowered him to speak his truth while also assessing the impact of that within relationships with his parents and peers. He advocated for his rights to play on the boys' soccer team and while he wasn't successful in that endeavor, the process helped him to find his voice.

For me, this case study demonstrates the power of connection with our equine partners. Particularly when working at liberty where the horses have the choice to engage or not, clients experience profound insights into their inner lives and are able to increase their awareness of how they enter relationships with others. This way of working in the present moment, attending to the meaning that clients make for themselves, without inserting our own interpretations of their experience, and allowing the relationship between client and horse to emerge is foundational to The HERD Institute® approach. This example also highlights the importance of cultural competence when working with marginalized youth. Our ability to honor their reality, their truth, and their choices about themselves while staying educated on the cultural context that forms the background of their lives is critical to the process. In this way, practitioners can become part of the solution for our underrepresented communities and help to challenge, change, and create a brave new world where everyone can belong.

Chapter 26

We've Already Entered Without Knocking

by Elizabeth McCorvey, LCSW

I read this insane tweet the other day by Dr. Autumn Asher BlackDeer.[1] It says: "You cannot decolonize diversity, equity, and inclusion. DEI is from a reformist paradigm (we can look to abolition to see why reform never works). Decolonization is from a paradigm of dismantling structures of oppression, not reforming them. DEl is operating exactly as intended." [2]

WHEW, ya'll! I don't have answers about what to do with that, so don't look to this chapter to figure it out. I'm in the muck with you. It resonates deeply, though, particularly as someone who does a lot of diversity, equity, and inclusion (DEI) work with individuals and organizations. If you know me, you know that I'm a bit of a conundrum: I'm a psychotherapist who doesn't believe in psychotherapy as a long-term solution for community wellness. When community needs are met, the need for psychotherapy decreases. That's what I'm working toward. In my work as an equine-facilitated therapist, I've witnessed how bringing horses into the conversation can lay the foundation for transformative ways of being together. We know (or we think we know) that horses are particularly skilled at negotiating space, communicating without words, and sharing power. If we're really paying attention, we can see outside of the power and dominance archetype and notice the subtle ways horses trade opportunities for leadership and co-create a collective culture. To that end, I don't turn to my horse teachers to figure out how to reform a system that wasn't built for us and doesn't serve us. I'm trying to learn how to create a community that is anti-colonial, radically loving, accepting, and

---

[1] Dr. Autumn Asher BlackDeer identifies as a decolonial indigiqueer scholar–activist from the Southern Cheyenne Nation.
[2] BlackDeer, A. [@drblackdeer]. (2023, February 3). Retrieved from https://twitter.com/DrBlackDeer/status/ 1621502213796552704.

compassionate. I'm learning how to belong to a herd where boundaries are clear and everyone has a felt sense of inclusion and belonging.

I often think about the barriers we've put in the horse's way to creating community. We've stolen their land, so we have to tell them where they can eat, and how much. We took away their ability to roam, so we tell them when they must work or rest. We sold their friends and family, so they have to find new ones with whom to socialize, perhaps with herd mates that they wouldn't choose for themselves. We force them to learn our language in order to communicate. Sound familiar? These practices are the backbone of the history of the United States. "Horses are so adaptable," you might say, but I might disagree. I look back into my own familial background where there's stolen land and stolen language and stolen community. Are we adaptable and resilient, or simply determined to survive? All of the above? Either way, the circumstances of forced assimilation are traumatizing. In order to learn how to live, we first learned how not to die.[3]

The trauma of surviving in a society that wants you dead is reflected in our bloodlines. Epigenetics is the research that captures how chronic stress changes our cellular structure and is passed down from generation to generation. Put simply, we carry traumas in our lineage and are impacted by them on a cellular level. In the same way, the horse that was captured from their homeland four thousand years ago is reflected in the horse that is standing in front of you today. We cannot be separated from our history. What has followed in our society is an outcasting of those who carry the scars of genocide, of those who could not assimilate in the "right" way. Marginalization occurs when groups of people are systematically excluded or disenfranchised due to a socially constructed status quo. By most definitions of the term, horses qualify as being a marginalized population. Further, the term "forced marginalized" or "marginalized by force" applies to communities of people (or horses) who have been cast out, minoritized, and oppressed due to the impacts of capitalism, white supremacy and Western dominance. The term "forced" in this context is important because it highlights the external and avoidable pressures that have led to this outcome, putting the onus where it belongs: on those in power. If you believed that horses are continually impacted by colonialism and that their relationships with us are informed by historical and present

---

[3] Taylor, K. (2017). How we get free: Black feminism and the Combahee River Collective.

trauma, would you change the way you interacted with them? Would it change the way you interact with people who look like me?

One of my many side hustles is working with groups of humans who want to bring an anti-oppressive lens into their workspaces. This means examining DEI principles and acknowledging the influences of white supremacy culture. I used to do this in a conference room with PowerPoint (boring), but doing this alongside horses has breathed new life into the work. So now, I cut out the PowerPoint and bring people out to the barn to meet my sweet horses, and it's way more fun and interesting for all of us. The themes that come up with my little herd are similar, DEI group or not; if I had a dollar for every time someone said, "I want to go up to them and say hi but I want to respect their space," I'd have a lot of dollars. My clients share that they are hesitant to approach because they see the horses eating or standing in their stalls, and they don't want to be disruptive by potentially breaching their boundaries. Here's how the conversation usually goes:

> "I don't want to get into their space," my client says, watching the horses graze. Their body leans forward, but they don't move their feet. "I want to go say hi, but I think I'll wait for them to come up to me."

> "We're already in their space," I remind them. "We've already entered their room without knocking."

> My client looks at me, and then looks back to the horse. "Oh. I hadn't thought about it that way."

> I pause, watching them watch the horse. "I think about that a lot. It's a big request for us to enter their space without asking and then also make them do the emotional labor of approaching us first."

My clients then make whatever decisions feel in alignment for them or draw the parallels that pop up for their own lives—about being an outsider, about being intruded upon, about being in a position of dominance. It's always a rich conversation, and a sobering reminder for those of us who partner with horses: No matter how much work we do, we'll never be 100% sure we have the horse's consent to work with them. And yet, we do it anyway. For the DEI groups, I take it a step further: I tell them that the beauty of doing this work with horses is that we get to examine how they approach a marginalized group because the horses *are* a marginalized group. We took the land that belonged to the horse and then returned to them a portion of it, corrupted and with strings attached. Like the city that participates in gentrification of Black communities and then gives the streets names like "Martin Luther King Blvd." Like starting a presentation with a land acknowledgement, without specifically naming that the land was stolen. "This is Treska's paddock," I say. Until I decide it's not. Our existence has always historically precluded their freedom.

I phrase it this way to my clients: "The way you choose to approach my horses can be indicative of how you approach oppressed populations. What do you want to do with that knowledge?" I ask them. When the group I'm working with is primarily Black, Indigenous, and people of color, they resonate deeply. We know what it's like to have public lives; being colonized is in our DNA. Everyone approaches the horses more thoughtfully after that. From an equine-facilitated-practitioner perspective, it's not often that I assign my own agenda to my clients. I'm willing to have this particular agenda, though, because I think it's that important. I'm already a willing participant in the colonial domination of a species, so to hide that knowledge does an enormous disservice to my DEI work.

Humans are dominant in this relationship, and our will has always taken precedent. We must hold that fact gently, with both hands. One of my horses, Treska, is a 17.2-foot, half-Clydesdale tank. His hooves are dinner plates, and he towers over people like a small elephant. When I ask people their initial impressions of him, they say, "He's intimidating," "He's confident," "He's big and scary," "He isn't interested in me." Treska regularly gets this kind of feedback. I wonder how it impacts him. People tiptoe up to him and interact timidly. My heart connects with this. I know what it's like for people to know nothing about me and be afraid of me because of how I look. They see me as the threat, even when they have centuries of power on their side. This might get me shot one day.

The story I tell myself about Treska is this: The dude is petrified. He often chooses to take his own space away from people, but I don't think it's because he's afraid of connection. I think he quite enjoys connection, but a prey animal connecting with a predator always comes with the risk of being hurt—not a matter of if, but when. That's true for me, too. To watch me speak publicly about diversity, equity, and inclusion, you would not know that I am terrified. I can give you facts and data and confidently offer challenges, but behind all of that I'm asking, "Do you believe me? Would you still love me if you did? Will you cast me out of your community if I make you face yourself? Do you see me?"

Horses are marginalized in a public way, to the extent that their sovereign bodies are discussed in terms of ownership. In a parallel way, people who are shackled to carceral systems live public lives that belong to the people who are tasked with managing them. This includes families who have involvement with social services, people who are incarcerated or on parole, people who immigrated across invisible borders, people who are unhoused, hospitalized...the list goes on. People who are beholden to societal expectations are aware of the publicity of their lives as well: Transgender individuals endure questions about "the surgery," what their dead name was, the gender they were assigned at birth. Visibly pregnant people have strangers put hands on their bodies and are asked intrusive questions about the cells growing inside of them. People speaking different languages might face assault by someone who says, "You're in America; speak English!" When you are marginalized in a public way, people in power enact ownership over your private life. Horses know this. When a horse protests an injustice by raising their voice, they are often punished. Black, Indigenous and people of color Americans know this.

My relationship with horses is constantly evolving. Like many of you, I learned how to work with horses through the lens of the power dynamic. Unlearning those lessons is hard! I'm forever exploring what mutual respect might mean to my horses, and how to fully embody a culture of consent when I need their compliance to rectify the issues our human culture created. I'm certain that having these conversations with Treska will unlock some clues as to how to divest from colonialism and explore egalitarian ways of being together... I'll let you all know when I figure out exactly how to do that. Luckily, as with any healthy relationship, I don't think Treska needs me to get it right 100% of the time. My job is to keep asking questions, and I have plenty of those.

Lilla Watson, who was in community with the Aboriginal Rights group, is quoted as saying, "If you have come here to help me, you are wasting your time. But if you have come because your liberation is bound up with mine, then let us work together." Similarly, the Combahee River Collective challenged us in 1977 to consider that if we can liberate Black lesbian women, we can unlock liberation for everyone. When we consider the needs of the least of us, we can support the most of us. Although there's plenty I'm figuring out, I think the answer to "How do we make things right in this society for the humans?" will be the same as the answer to "How do we make it right for the horses?"

I'm not advocating that we set all of the horses free; the ship has sailed on that one. Through selective breeding and land theft, we've made it impossible for them to return home. But I think if we start listening a little more closely to the marginalized populations we're connected to, we can figure out how to "dismantle the structures of oppression," as Dr. BlackDeer invites in the quote at the beginning of this chapter, instead of trying to reform something that had a broken premise from the beginning. To do so, we would need to explore radical compassion, to radically see each other, and offer radical understanding to one another. I'm working on doing this in my herds of humans, horses, and colleagues. What's your herd dynamic?

Chapter 27

Seeing Differences

by Rachael Loucks

Shonda was a 13-year-old African American girl who was homeschooled. Her Black father remarried a white woman, and they live in a community that is primarily white and conservative where the predominant view regarding race is that "All lives matter," and the Black Lives Matter movement is viewed as being racist toward white people. Discussions of white privilege will quickly be shut down with comments from whites on how difficult their own lives are, and the only white privilege that exists is if you're part of the Shield family who own the biggest business in town.

Shonda did well in school and appeared to have a strong relationship with her dad and stepmom. In our intake session, her stepmom indicated that Shonda suffered from severe social anxiety and often felt isolated from her peers. She was hoping that Shonda could have some interactions with folks outside her immediate family and find ways to connect with her African American heritage. The overall aim for Shonda was to learn how to ask for support, increase her confidence in social settings, and build on some social skills to help her make friends. In our weekly sessions, Shona primarily worked with Kohl, an 18-year-old Paint mare, but sometimes partnered with Princess, one of the minis on our farm.

In this session, we were working with Princess, and we began with Shonda selecting a halter and lead rope for Princess and going out to the paddock to bring her in. In our previous session, Shonda learned how to halter Kohl and tie a quick release knot. She was able to demonstrate the skills of approaching horses in the paddock, haltering, and leading independently, which she did once again this time. When it came to tying the quick release knot at the hitching post, Shonda made two attempts before looking at me and asked if I would come and check her knot, saying "I don't remember how to do it."

We practiced a few times together before she tried it again on her own. "I did it!", she said, smiling up at me. "What's that like for you, that you did it?" I asked. "It was hard, but I kept trying. It was cool to finally, get it" she said with a grin. "I'm so glad you were able to ask for help when you needed it, too," I said. With that, I invited Shonda to gather the grooming supplies she wanted to use. She looked at the selection of grooming tools and picked a mix of soft and hard brushes, a hoof pick, and the fly spray. She identified which brushes are safe for legs, good for removing hard dirt, and which were safe for the face. As we looked through some of the brushes, I held out a firm, curry brush made of a hard rubber and asked, "What do you think it might be like for Princess if you brushed her on the legs or face with this brush?" Shonda rubbed the brush on her arm, elbows, and knuckles and said, "I don't think Princess will like it. It feels good in some places but not on my bony bits. I don't think we should use it on her legs. Maybe just on her fleshy parts." I asked her how she might know if Princess didn't like how or where she was being brushed. Shonda considered this for a moment. "Princess might put her ears back, turn and give me the stink eye, or swish her tail. I think she'd give me the stink eye if she's annoyed with me or mad," she said. "What about you? How do you tell people if you don't like what's going on, or if you're mad?" I asked. Chuckling quietly, she said, "I use the stink eye sometimes, too!"

As Shonda began to pick one of her hooves, Princess pulled her leg away. Shonda immediately stepped away. Princess stood quietly again. "What do you make of that?" I asked. "Maybe it hurts her when I pick her hooves," she replied. "How do you think we should proceed now?" I asked. "Let's finish picking her hooves because there might be something wrong. We need to look at her hooves more" said Shonda, frowning a little as she spoke. I asked how she thought we could do that, mindful of creating a safe space for her and Princess. Shonda asked if I would demonstrate how to pick one of Princess' hooves, and asked if we needed to do something different because Princess is so small. "Hmm...good question, Shonda" I said, "I like that you're paying attention to how to keep you both safe and comfortable."

As I lifted the hoof that Shonda had started to pick, I noticed the beginning signs of some thrush. I showed Shonda the hoof, confirming that she was right, and that Princess may indeed be experiencing some discomfort. I explained what thrush is and how we treat it. We also brainstormed some ways we could support Princess when we are picking her hooves. "What might we need to do differently with Princess compared to Kohl?" I asked. Shonda stated that she noticed that Princess seemed to like it better when we held her leg lower to the ground, instead of picking her leg up high like she had done with Kohl previously. "What are you noticing right now?" I asked, as she continued to attend to Princess. "She's not pulling her leg away anymore, and she isn't swishing her tail. And she isn't turning around to give me the stink eye!"

Once we'd completed the task, Shonda asked if we could take Princess for a walk up the driveway to graze a little. As we walked, I asked her, "What do you think it's like for Princess when we pay attention to how she has different needs than Kohl?" Shonda smiled, "I bet it makes her want to hang out with us more. I noticed she doesn't run away from me now when I go and halter her. Maybe she thinks I'm listening to her now." Shonda explained that she often felt different from everyone else around her, but rarely has a chance to explain what that's like for her, and that it's difficult to feel like the odd one out. "I hear you. What are you experiencing right now?" I asked. "I feel better just saying that to someone. Princess heard me, like when I listened to her. She knows what it's like to be different, too."

This case study demonstrates the importance of working from a cultural competence framework, understanding the challenges and isolation that Black, Indigenous, and people of color in rural communities often face. Themes of physical and emotional safety emerged in the session as Shonda navigated how to ask for support initially with the quick release knot, as well as in the moment of her stepping out of harm's way as Princess pulled her leg back. These embodied experiences of being met in moments of uncertainty and/or fear are critical for Black youth living in predominantly white spaces. Modeling a relational way of being with the horses also helped Shonda to feel seen and heard by me and Princess. If we'd focused only on the task at hand and ignored Princess' reluctance to lift her hoof, we may have inadvertently reinforced Shonda's experiences of not being heard, while simultaneously replicating society's acceptance of dominance over others. Instead, in centering Shonda's meaning of her experience with Princess, she was able to speak her truth and feel heard. This is particularly important within a community of "All Lives Matter" rhetoric, where racial differences will likely also be dismissed through microaggressive comments of "I don't see color," "We're all part of the human race," and "You might be Black, but you're just like us." Allowing space for Black youth like Shonda to identify with and claim her Blackness so that she can take pride in her differences can help to reduce the impact of the racialized trauma in her everyday life.

Chapter 28

What a "Safe Space" Looks Like: Fostering Diversity and Inclusion Through Authenticity and Visibility

by Ellen Lichtenstein

It feels strange to be writing about diversity, equity, and inclusion. Most people who see me peg me for a straight, white, cisgender woman without any disabilities. And that's a perception I've passively accepted throughout my life. Sometimes because I was ashamed to be seen as anything other than perfectly "normal" even when I knew I wasn't. Sometimes because my identity was complicated (even to me) and still evolving, and I didn't know how to express it. And sometimes because it simply wasn't safe to correct the assumptions people made. "If they learned the truth about me," I thought, "I could lose a job, a relationship, or worse."

I recognize the immense privilege I hold compared to people of color, people who are more visibly queer or trans, and people with disabilities they can't hide from public view. My privilege is that I don't have to disclose these things if I don't want to. I've always understood this privilege and been grateful for it, but at the same time felt my identities could easily go unrecognized and unappreciated because they were so easily hidden. The double-edged sword of what some refer to as "passing privilege" is identity erasure.

That's why, when I became self-employed in 2020, I started making efforts to come out of the various closets I'd been keeping myself in. The truth is, I'm not a straight, white, cisgender woman without any disabilities. Only the "white" part is accurate, and even then, not if you ask a white supremacist. I'm 100% Ashkenazi Jew (according to both 23andMe and my bubbes[1]). It might be easy for some to forget that

---

[1] Yiddish word for grandparents

antisemitism still exists in America, but not for this Alabama-born Jew who grew up knowing there were places you didn't stop for gas.

The reality is I'm a pansexual, genderqueer, transmasculine woman with anxiety, post-traumatic stress disorder, sensory issues, and obsessive–compulsive disorder that have been severe enough to limit my daily ability to function at times. I'm also well educated, neurotypical passing, and an expert at disguising each of these identities. So much so that I've often made it through years at a job without anyone knowing me on more than a superficial level.

When I left the corporate world to start my own company, it no longer made sense to hide. Not only was it not doing me any good to keep my identities under wraps: I realized I couldn't build the type of equine-facilitated learning practice I wanted unless I showed up fully and authentically. I started realizing that just being visibly "me"—in all its complexity—was in itself a way to build a diverse and inclusive community. I remembered all the people I'd encountered in my life who proudly showed up as themselves, and in doing so helped me discover who I was and know that I wasn't alone. Those people gave me words for what I felt on the inside. I realized that visibility can be allyship, and I realized I needed to be visible for myself and for others.

It's fair to say that I formed strong bonds with horses and other animals as a child because they were the only relationships I had access to that allowed me to be myself. I grew up in an environment where criticism was endless and perfection was expected but unachievable. Whether it was based on a physical characteristic, a psychological quirk, or any other shortcoming, my mother (a single parent) and my school-aged peers didn't hesitate to remind me daily how I didn't fit in or measure up.

With horses, along with dogs, cats, mice, hamsters, rabbits, and anything else I could sneak home as a child, I found my first healthy interactions. These animals laid the foundation for relationships built on who I am, not what I can provide, or how much I can achieve. It was a foundation that was buried under trauma and would take 30 years to emerge as my new reality. But without my early relationships with horses, I might never have come out the other side. Or at least it would have cost a lot more in therapy than it did.

If you're reading this, you likely don't question the mental and even spiritual benefits that come from relationships with our equine partners. When you think about some of these benefits, do they include trust, understanding, love, self-expression, peace, and acceptance?

These are just a few of the things I can say I felt from my relationships with horses as a child and adolescent, and still feel today. They're valuable *and vital* for every single human, yet most people experience some of these things (maybe even all of them) solely through their parents, family, and friends. Plenty of people grow up without horses and turn out just fine.

But what about youth with disabilities, neurodivergence, genders that are incongruent with their physical bodies, people who are racial or ethnic minorities or otherwise not a part of the dominant culture in the United States? For people who experience stigma, isolation, racism, sexism, homophobia, transphobia, and more (often in multiple layers), the chance to relate to horses may be—as it was for me—one of the only avenues to fulfill these pivotal emotional needs.

Authenticity as Allyship

I started my equine-facilitated learning (EFL) practice with the intention of working with corporate teams like the ones I'd been a part of for 15 years in my professional career. While trying to build that side of the practice, I also offer riding lessons since my horses are well suited for it, and I've been teaching children and beginners to ride since I was a teenager. When I became certified in EFL through The HERD Institute, I incorporated EFL principles into my teaching to the point that I can't truly differentiate what is a "riding lesson" versus mounted EFL anymore.

Regarding The HERD Institute, I shouldn't gloss over the fact that my introduction was via a conversation with Dr. Lac in which she told me "Diversity, equity, and inclusion are baked into our philosophy." This simple statement is what made me take my first look at the website, apply for EFL Level 1 training, and end up where I am today. There have been multiple times over the past few years that I've had the opportunity to share something vulnerable about myself with other members of The HERD community, and I've felt safe enough to do so. That's saying a lot for someone who never felt safe in human herds. What's even more significant to me is the way in which each vulnerability has been received. My experience as a student in this community further cemented my quest to provide the same for students who come to me. I have since completed my EFL Level 2 training and am currently in training to become an EFL instructor. My commitment to this journey and The HERD community is supported by my deep sense of belonging in this space. Intentional inclusion is impactful.

Inclusion in Action at Leg-Up Learning Solutions

As it happened, my lesson program grew larger than I anticipated. And, most surprising (or not?), many of my students are from under-represented and under-resourced populations. I have autistic clients with sensory processing disorders, clients with non-binary genders, and clients from LGBTQIA families. I haven't gone looking for these folks, who happen to have a lot in common with me, yet they've found me. The only thing I've done is work to be more and more authentically myself, and in doing so create an environment where a diverse set of clients feel welcome and included.

If you asked me how to create an inclusive program, I wouldn't be able to give you a playbook. For me, being very honest about who I am has created a place where people with whatever differences, even if they don't mirror my own, tell me they feel comfortable and accepted. What I can do, however, is describe some of the impacts on clients I've seen through my program's intentional focus on diversity, equity, and inclusion. I'll focus on two students whose names have been changed to preserve anonymity.

Mae
Mae came to me as a three-year-old and has been taking weekly lessons for just over a year. At our first lesson, Mae's mom made mention of her wife, which took me by surprise. I didn't have any assumptions about the family one way or the other, but statistically speaking I figured chances were better that Mae had a mom and dad rather than two moms. This just goes to show how, even as members of marginalized groups, we still hold our own biases—often shaped by the dominant culture even if we feel disconnected from it.

Once the door had been opened, I felt comfortable sharing my own non-binary gender and overall queer identity. This was still earlier in my ever-evolving journey, and I was more cautious about who I came out to, due to the very real fear that a client might be less than friendly to people under the LGBTQIA rainbow. While I wasn't very forward with talking about these things in person at the time, my website bio has reflected my "she or they" pronouns from day one, giving me hope that clients who "don't believe in trans people" will find another place to go before they even contact me.

As soon as I told Mae's mom that I was also queer and genderqueer, she shared how happy they were to have found me after visiting several barns and getting a feeling their family "wouldn't be welcome" there. I knew exactly what she meant. Colorado isn't Alabama, but regardless of the geography, the equestrian world contains a wide range of people with numerous ways to signpost that queer families aren't embraced.

Everyday Obstacles and Challenges for Queer Families

Even in a best case scenario, where an environment appears to be LGBTQIA friendly, straight people may not realize how burdensome it is for us to constantly correct pronouns, explain our family structure, or answer questions like "Which one of you is the man in the relationship?" Other microaggressions (and full-on aggressions) I've heard within the horse world include people misgendering trans folks or refusing to use gender neutral pronouns and terminology. For example, the constant "Hey, ladies!" greeting even when the intended audience includes a non-binary or trans person, and it's been repeatedly made clear that "ladies" isn't an appropriate reference. Even something as seemingly innocent as asking a woman what her husband does is a constant reminder to a woman with a female partner that this world isn't made for her.

"I get so tired of coming out over and over again," Mae's mom told me. "Sometimes I just say, 'website developer' and let them assume my wife is a man because it's easier than correcting the assumption."

If you're cisgender, straight, white, and able-bodied, you likely take it for granted that you can walk into a new environment without getting questions that make you explain your identity. This is a stark contrast from the experience of someone who's met with stares and whispers of, "Is that a boy or a girl?" each time they enter a new space. Think about how nice it must be for a family to show up for riding lessons with both moms or a queer or trans kid and know that they won't have to explain anything. This is a luxury straight families get in everyday situations yet can be a real obstacle for queer families who want to access the same services and spaces. By being authentic about my identity, even if it makes me feel vulnerable at times, my clients know they don't have to spend any time or energy bracing themselves for judgment or inappropriate questions.

Impact and Outcomes

Throughout our time together, I've had the privilege of watching Mae learn so much more than how to groom, tack up, and steer her horse. Don't get me wrong, she's a horse-crazy kid if there ever was one! Apparently, she talks about horses (specifically Icelandic horses, thanks to me and my herd) nonstop. She's already decided that she wants to jump, do dressage, race, *and* that she'll be a riding instructor when she grows up.

However, the benefits of her lessons go well beyond satisfying her horse addiction:

- Physically, she's grown by leaps and bounds in her strength and motor skills. I see her holding the reins correctly, she's able to steer her horse through cones independently, and she's physically able to handle her horse moving more quickly, even when she's surprised by an unexpected speed or direction change.
- Emotionally, she's gained self-regulation skills and is now more likely to speak about what she wants, rather than to screech or cry.
- She's gained confidence and independence, as evidenced by her newfound willingness to ride through the neighborhood without her mother nearby when she once was glued to mom at the hip.

Each of these progressions aren't outside of the norm or unexpected for a small child as she grows and develops. But they're achievements Mae might have missed out on, or delayed having, if her parents were unable to find a riding program they felt comfortable with.

"Horses and riding are something she's truly in love with and it's sparked a passion for learning in her. She can't get enough and wants to learn more about horses every day." Mae's mom says, "There were a lot of places we looked at and I just knew, frankly, we wouldn't feel safe there. That's why we don't even question driving 45 minutes each way to ride here."

Luma
Luma is a gender non-binary nine-year-old with sensory processing disorder, anxiety disorder, and currently being evaluated for ADHD and/or autism. While they came to my practice because they'd been

begging their mother to ride horses for years, the work we've done reaches far beyond learning to ride a horse. In a typical lesson, Luma gets to practice and improve upon their social skills, critical thinking, emotional awareness and regulation, personal boundaries, and *of course*, interpersonal, and interspecies relationships.

In their daily life, Luma faces a lot of peer-based bullying and mistreatment at school. During our lessons, they've told me how kids at school will say things like "You don't look like a girl because you have short hair and girls are supposed to have long hair." Or "You're not allowed to wear a suit. Where's your dress?" But at riding lessons, these simply aren't things they have to think about.

I recently asked Luma what it was like for them to ride with me, knowing I'm also non-binary and they don't have to think about, explain, or justify their identity here. They shrugged and just said, "Horses are great therapists." I didn't think it was the right time or place to go into the finer details of how EFL differs from EFP.

Luma's mother chimed in. "Being around you and the horses gives Luma a space to navigate their anxiety. When we're out in the world and they get anxious, we often stop to think about the horses: what it feels like to ride, how soft their manes are. It's a great tool for breaking the anxiety cycle. The way you ask Luma a lot of questions and let them make choices about which horse to ride, which saddle to use, and what activities to do is a rare opportunity for them to express agency in a world where they're often pushed from place to place."

Hearing this feedback from Luma's mother affirms my belief that I'm not just teaching Luma how to ride a horse, but truly practicing EFL based on the HERD principles I've studied.

Here's an example of how the HERD principles of *here and now*, *what and how*, and *I and thou* come into my lessons with Luma:

Here and Now
Luma is riding Helo. He's a 22-year-old gelding with saintly patience who just came home from spending two years working at a PATH therapeutic riding center. Helo will put up with nearly anything and doesn't always broadcast his opinions loudly, so I pay special attention to gauging where he's at during any lesson he's part of.

As they walk around the arena, Luma chats nonstop about their usual random topics. I notice they aren't stopping to take breaths between sentences. I also notice their legs are moving sporadically all over Helo's barrel. Their hands are busy flipping the slack part of the reins back and forth, pointing the buckle toward Helo's withers and back toward the saddle repeatedly. I find myself "zooming in and out" as I focus on their specific body movements and then the bigger picture. Is Luma at risk of falling? Are there any other imminent safety issues? I ask myself these questions and find the answers almost instinctively after so many years of teaching children to ride.

Then I scan Helo. I look at his eyes and face, his headset, then at the entire picture. I notice he isn't showing any true signs of distress, but I know his rider's movements aren't comfortable, and he shouldn't have to patiently deal with it for the rest of the lesson. Not least of all, I'm teaching riding lessons, and this isn't the way you ride a horse.

What and How

I ask Luma to stop for a minute so we can talk about what's going on. I tell them that I notice they're moving a lot and ask them what's going on for them. Luma says they're anxious because of some upcoming events and the start of a new school year.

I mention that Luma's hands are doing a lot of moving and I ask them what they think Helo might think of that movement. Luma concludes that Helo might not like it and apologizes to him. I ask Luma if they need to get off the horse and get a bunch of energy out; they say no, they just need to stand quietly for a minute, so we do.

I and Thou

In my opinion, the I–Thou moments are happening throughout everything I've previously described. Luma and I are being entirely present with one another. Luma feels seen when I bring attention to what's going on with their body and give them a chance to put words to what's happening internally. Luma and Helo are also being there for each other, as Helo doesn't object to their jitters, so they can feel safe to exist as they are. But at the same time, Luma can recognize the potential impact of their movement on Helo and have empathy for any discomfort they might have caused. In this one small example, spanning a matter of minutes, I believe Luma, Helo, and I were all feeling seen and supported.

I don't know how Luma would have fared at the kind of riding schools I spent time at as a kid. I can imagine anything from their pronouns being disregarded to being told they couldn't ride until they "learned to control themselves." I don't run a therapeutic riding center, nor do I claim to. But my deep understanding of the issues my clients deal with daily allows me to create an atmosphere where they know they're not being judged, and real learning can occur.

It's About Equal Access, Not Special Treatment

As I write these accounts of my students and what they've gained from our riding lessons (or mounted EFL if you prefer), nothing strikes me as extraordinary. The benefits they get are the same as others, regardless of race, gender, sexual orientation, or disability.

And that's exactly the point.

To achieve "equal" outcomes—that is, for a marginalized person to achieve the same results or feel the same impact as a non-marginalized person—we often need to provide something different. We can't offer the same thing in different environments and expect the same outcomes. Cultural sensitivity and competency are crucial. Diversity, equity, and inclusion are not about providing *special* treatment to marginalized groups. It's about understanding that there are differences so that we can adjust to what is needed to create an equitable experience for those populations because of historic inequalities and disparities. In the case of my students, that different element can be as "simple" as me being wholly and authentically myself when they show up. By doing so, I give them the ability to safely be *who they are.* Speaking from experience, that's not something many I work with can take for granted.

My goal, my intention, is to create a practice where people who walk through the world with the weight of historical marginalization, oppression, and judgment can feel the freedom they deserve. I want them to feel what it's like to be themselves and not have anyone ask what's wrong with them or point out how they don't fit into a societal norm. Believe me, we know! And we'd love for once to experience what it's like not to be reminded of our differences in every interaction in a way that creates distance rather than inclusion.

The greatest gift horses can give us is permission to show up as we are, without hiding who we are. By striving to create an inclusive EFL practice, we can extend that gift to the people who need it the most.

Chapter 29

When There Are No Words

by Dr. Danielle Mills

Several of my clients have been labelled with selective mutism; this often co-occurs with autism and other neurodivergent conditions. It feels important to begin this chapter by challenging the language of "selective mutism" (SM) as well as exploring the process by which this behaviour occurs. I am going to use the term SM throughout this chapter as I do not yet have a better term to use as shorthand; I am very open to further discussion about this. Labels can often be a useful way to communicate a shared understanding of behaviours as well as to signpost community spaces, so it could arguably be important to find a more suitable label to ensure that continuity.

Clients with SM tend to struggle with communicating verbally due to extreme anxiety. This is selective mutism, but it is important to note that this is not a *choice* for them: When they are anxious, they will be physically unable to speak due to experiencing an intense trauma response. With SM, it is likely that someone may be in a nervous system state that does not support cognition, so they are simply not able to access the prefrontal cortex. The prefrontal cortex (PFC) is critical for cognition and speech. A parent of one my clients uses the term "situational mutism" when they're talking to someone who doesn't understand SM in an attempt to communicate that their family member is not choosing when and where to speak out of stubbornness, rudeness, or shyness.

Referring agencies will often talk about a "lack of communication" from these clients. I invite them to consider what they mean when they talk about lack of communication: Is it that they are more specifically referring to a lack of speaking? We need to challenge the neurotypical concept that non-speaking equals non-communication. This is where there is a parallel in collaborating with horses and other non-human animals.

Non-Speaking and Non-Verbal Communication

Working with horses requires a very different way of communicating and relating. Horses are also non-speaking, but this does not mean that they don't communicate. Far from it! Noticing and exploring how horses communicate with other horses, as well as with humans, can help us to reflect on what this means, what meaning we make of this, and how we respond. The language of the horse operates through the body such that horses must use their bodies to communicate their subjective presence because humans cannot convey intentions to horses through spoken language. Suggesting that the body can be a basis for language challenges the privileged status of speech in the neurotypical world.

This also invites us as facilitators to notice and explore how our human clients are communicating in non-speaking ways, what this means, what meaning we make of this, and how we respond. Being curious about this is an important step towards beginning to understand the client's phenomenological (i.e., meaning making) experience of the world. We again need to remove the neurotypical lens by recognizing that *any* communication from the client is significant; shrugs, head shakes, gestures, and nods should be given equal weight as it may be hard for someone to do even that. I would also recommend that we question the assumption that a lack of eye contact means that a person is not listening. From listening to feedback from neurodivergent folks, we know that this is not necessarily the case. In fact, it is often the case that if a neurodivergent client feels the expectation of maintaining eye contact, that they are not able to simultaneously process the information being given. Eye contact does not equal listening and engagement, and we don't need to make people make eye contact.

When a client's nervous system shuts down and their communication is highly restricted, such as in dissociation, we may benefit from supporting the client to co-regulate and get back into a more relaxed or neutral state. We also cannot expect them to do this alone. We often see the term "self-regulation" used with therapies purporting to build client capacity to do this. It is important to note that we cannot even begin to think about self-regulation until someone has learned to co-regulate.

Dissociation and Upregulation

Poppy is currently unable to attend secondary school due to her extreme anxiety. Poppy has been very clear that education is important to her, and that she wants to attend and do well academically. She has tried to get into school, but her trauma response is such that she engages in serious self-harm—including trying to get out of the moving vehicle on the way to school. Poppy initially accessed equine-facilitated psychotherapy with me in the hope of being able to attend school education again but has been unable to do so despite multiple attempts. Again, it is important to note that this is not a choice, but a result of intense dysregulation. The prefrontal cortex, or cognitive part, of Poppy's brain wants to be able to do this, but her nervous system initiates an extreme response to get out of the situation and survive. This can be referred to as the "fight" response; a fight trauma response is characterized by the unconscious need to escape pain, emotional turmoil, and other distress.

When Poppy first came to therapy, she presented as being able to talk quite freely about her interests. Poppy is autistic and she is passionately interested in animals. When exploring co-regulation with these clients, I try to find out their safe topics and engage in conversation about their interests in order to build rapport with them. Showing a sincere attentiveness in their interests is really important since it is often the experience of autistic people that they are not allowed to talk about what they feel passionate about, as this typically is perceived as poor social skills. I want to provide them with a non-judgmental space to speak passionately about what interests them. I feel honored when people feel safe enough to tell me all about what they love! Engaging clients in "safe talk" can help with upregulation of the nervous system that is essential for social interactions.

It is also important to note, however, that in some cases the engagement in safe talk may also represent an initial "fawn" response that is rooted in clients' conditioned responses to behave as they believe that they "should." In Poppy's case, when this happens, I focus on working with her so that she is more able to spend time with me and the horses while choosing not to speak, and instead explore communication methods that she is more comfortable with. This may include writing notes, texting, or simple sign language.

From a self-awareness perspective for the facilitator, it is important that I can reflect on why Poppy is not talking: Is she choosing not to talk, dissociating, or entering an unsafe nervous system state? This requires me to access my felt sense of the situation, as well as pay attention to how the horses are responding to us, as often I will experience bodily sensations, and/or shifts in energy that may alert me to shifts in my clients. I often experience Poppy as being quite shut down in sessions, frozen in place but not present. Co-regulation is important here, as well as being able to recognize micro-communications that signal moving in and out of trauma states. When someone is dissociating, we might consider upregulation through different interactions.

My three-year-old gelding, Jesus, is excellent at providing upregulation. I have observed that when Poppy is in the field with Jesus, he will interact with her in a way that helps to orient her in the here and now. It has taken some time for Poppy to be able to interact with the horses as she initially felt intimidated by their presence. As Poppy began to feel more confident with the horses, I noticed that in the moments when she appeared to downregulate (e.g., I would notice her looking at the ground, becoming silent and frozen in place), Jesus would often walk up and stand close to Poppy. His movements would be energetic and quick—sniffing, nudging, pawing the ground—alerting Poppy to his presence. Poppy would respond to these moments by upregulating to become more present and playful. These were moments of I–Thou relating that brought joy to her. She would laugh and engage with Jesus more freely.

During one session, Poppy was spending time grooming one of the mares, Coco. I noticed my excitement as Poppy began to groom as we'd worked so hard for her to overcome her hesitation in interacting through touch. I wondered how Poppy was feeling: Was she excited or scared? I couldn't tell, and I didn't want to interrupt this precious moment of connection by asking her. So, I simply observed her, breathing deeply to stay grounded for both of us. After a few minutes, I noticed Poppy beginning to slow her movements as she groomed, and her hand began to drop to her side. I understood this as an indication that she was beginning to dissociate. I was about to speak to get her attention when Jesus walked up to her and nudged her arm. Poppy took a breath and looked at Jesus. "Oh, you want to be groomed too?" she asked quietly. With that, she began to alternately brush Coco and Jesus, both of whom stood quietly at her side throughout the remainder of the session. Each time I noticed that she began to dissociate, Jesus would nudge her arm and bring her back to the present moment.

Being in an environment where we can practice co-regulation, upregulation, and down-regulation can help clients to develop a toolbox of skills and experiences that are transferable to other situations. This is the start of learning to self-regulate.

Projecting into the Void

I have worked with Ciara for several years now. Ciara has not attended education for many years due to the trauma that she experienced in school. Emotional-based school avoidance appears to be a consistent issue in the clients who have experienced trauma within the school system. The expectations inherent in even special educational settings appear to demand a high level of masking[1] from neurodivergent clients, and this often has damaging long-term consequences. There also appears to be a huge pressure on students to learn to pass as neurotypical rather than being supported to explore and embrace their neurodivergent identities. A fundamental part of working within The HERD Model™ and the type of space that I endeavor to build is to support clients to become *more* of themselves, not less, and to feel safe to engage with me authentically.

It is interesting that it is precisely this process of allowing myself to be authentic and take up space that I struggle with when working with clients like Ciara. The data that I usually rely on when working with speaking clients is missing with clients with SM. I am left projecting into the void, which leaves me feeling insecure. I notice that I begin to question my skills as a facilitator; I wonder if the client is gaining any value from our sessions, and question whether I should refer them to someone who "knows what they are doing." I find that clinical supervision and personal therapy is key when working with this client group to be able to hold space for the client while experiencing this. Attending to my own self-awareness in these sessions can give me crucial information about how Ciara might feel as well as how other people might respond to her. I am also aware that the insecurity that this process elicits in me further drives a disconnection in relationship with Ciara.

Paying attention to how the horses respond to Ciara helps me to access an embodied sense of how she may be feeling in the relational space. When Ciara and I enter the field, I will observe how each of the horses are engaging with us, with one another, and with their

---

[1] I am using the term "masking" to refer to the different ways in which neurodivergent clients are conditioned to conform to neurotypical standards of behavior in social settings.

environment. Depending on Ciara's emotional state, she can sometimes reflect on this. There are also times when she is unable to. In these instances, rather than make assumptions about how she is feeling, I allow myself to stay curious: Is Ciara unable to process her thoughts to form an answer, unable to speak, or unable to respond at all? I can sometimes find myself working very hard to process this information in my attempts to form a response that Ciara can relate to. My growing edge is to regulate myself so that I can co-regulate with Ciara and the horses. As with all my clients, Ciara does not need fixing. She has been able to set firm boundaries to allow her to live her life in a way that addresses her needs; she has amazing resources to be able to thrive. My aim is not to get someone who is situationally mute to talk to me, but rather to feel safe in the space that we share.

At times, working within the school system, I am beholden to contracts and regulations that require support staff from the school to attend sessions with clients. In these instances, I make sure to brief the support staff on what a neurodivergent-affirmative approach means, and what it looks like in praxis.

When the children are with us, we need support staff to also be able to regulate themselves to help co-regulate the students. In this setting, we can offer the support staff some education on nervous system regulation techniques. Ultimately, I want us all to be able to embrace the idea that all behaviour is communication and offer a neurodiversity-affirming and trauma-informed provision. Within the school classroom environment, many of these clients are subjected to constant external sensory stimulus in an effort to distract them from behaviours that are deemed undesirable by the school system and staff. I feel that constantly engaging the students in activities to contain behaviour is not helpful in the long term. We want to build their capacity to deal with boredom and engage in activities that may feel uncertain to them. We can build this up gradually and ensure that there is extra support around transitions from one interaction to the next.

We offer a provision that supports students to be their authentic selves without masking for a neurotypical world, and this might mean exploring our tolerance levels as practitioners. If we are measuring the students by neurotypical standards of behaviour and engagement. then they will always fall short, and this will have a huge impact on their confidence and can be quite traumatising in the long term.

Relational Safety and Trust

As an equine-facilitated practitioner, it is imperative to be aware of your own process when working with clients with SM. By this, I mean that it is important to be aware of your own responses before, during, and after sessions. As with all clinical work, we need to be mindful of the transference and countertransference that occurs within a therapeutic encounter. We also need to be cognizant of how these processes are interconnected in the environment between ourselves, our client, and our horses. The greatest gift that we can offer our equine partners and our clients is our ability to co-regulate with them. This means that we need to have accumulated enough internal resources in our own lives to know how to self-regulate. When working with clients with SM, we also need to consider our own biases, particularly in privileging spoken language. When silence is present, it can be heavy with projections. By working within The HERD Model™ of phenomenological observations, catching ourselves in our interpretations and assumptions, we can be clear about the projections and stories we may be attributing to our clients who are unable to speak in those moments. Only then can we truly meet our clients where they need to be met, creating the relational safety and trust that is foundational to growth and healing.

Chapter 30

Care Enough to Care

by Naomi Nyamudoka

I have always felt different; even as a child I had a sense of being "other" in some way. Not because everyone treated me differently (though at times they very much did) but because I realised I seemed to react, think, and feel differently than those around me. When I was about eight years old, I devised a theory to try and explain this to myself. I called it "care enough to care." The basis of this theory was that instead of caring coming naturally to most people, they seemed to require some extra impetus in order to activate the caring; hence, "care enough to care."

As I grew older, I was told often that I was too much, too intense, an extremist. I became the person people would come to with their deeper worries and feelings, knowing that I wouldn't do any small talk or light chit chat. I spent my childhood trying to understand humans but preferring the company of animals, initially insects, particularly 'doosers' (my name for woodlice), then my dog, and when I was ten years old, two miniature Shetland ponies that I was asked to look after. For me, animals saw me and understood me. We spoke the same language. My feelings could flow freely, not requiring me to hide them in response to seeing how they landed on others, but rather were fully accepted and stepped towards. If I did something my animal friends didn't like, then I would know straight away; they would show me in their behaviour, which meant communication with them was so much easier for me than with the humans around me. I felt at home, at ease with my animals. I would spend hours just sitting in the field with my Shetlands, whilst all the other humans around me were focused on riding their horses, which at that time held no interest for me. What I was interested in was the communication, the shared connection, those moments when all that was felt was between my pony and me. Both of us noticing and responding to each other in moments which were so precious, what we would term in The HERD as I–Thou moments.

A lot of reflecting on why I have spent my life feeling like an alien in a landscape that others seem to fit into effortlessly finally led to my diagnosis of autism as an adult. I am autistic. I am not wrong, I am not extreme, I am not too much. I have a different neurotype from the majority of the population. My diagnosis was a huge moment for me and, although it has been a journey of acceptance and grief (not to mention overcoming some deep-rooted internalised ableism), it has been one of joy. I now have a reason why I find it so difficult to understand people's actions and communication, why others don't seem to be bothered by all the sensory things that I can find overwhelming, why I am able to notice the smallest changes in an environment that others seem unable to see, why detail and language matter so much to me, and why I need those around me to be explicit with their communication.

Does that sound familiar to you? As I have further explored my autistic self, I have noticed more and more the similarities in my needs in order to feel safe and unmasked to those of the equines I have known. Compared to many other mammals, horses have heightened senses and can detect changes easily. They notice detail and differences in environment, however small, and they thrive on routine and predictability, and appear to prefer humans to be explicit in what they are asking of them. I personally feel these similarities in how I experience the world and how it seems that horses experience the world are why being around them can feel easier for many autistic people.

I work with my herd of four, comprising two 28-year-old miniature Shetlands, Chip and Dale; a Welsh cob, Toby; and a Fell pony youngster, Dusk. I specialise in working with other neurodivergent, generally autistic, and ADHD adults, and adults who have experienced trauma. As those that work in this field may be aware, the brain changes due to trauma can mimic some of the behaviours you might see in a dysregulated autistic person. For example, your client might be hypervigilant, being very aware of everything going on around them and noticing the moment something changes. It is interesting to me doing this work that there are overlaps between the two; however ,there are also very important differences. For autistic clients this is not something that can change. For a client that has experienced trauma, this can change over time. This is a critically important distinction as, historically, autistic people have been consistently persecuted for being themselves. Indeed, there are brutal therapies still taking place around the world that directly harm autistic people in order to try to get them to behave in more neurotypical ways. Yes, this is possible, but the resulting damage is deeply traumatic and long term. Behaving like a neurotypical person should never be the goal of working with any autistic or neurodivergent person. For me, it's very much the opposite. When I am working with an autistic client, I want to encourage them to be more of themselves, bring out more of the ways they are in the world, to help them feel that they can find a space to unmask fully and be authentically themselves in the world. This is always my aim, and I have been very fortunate to witness some of my clients' journeys with this.

When I am working in an equine-facilitated psychotherapy setting with autistic clients, I will be mindful of letting them know expectations clearly. I will ensure I am being explicit in what to and what not to expect from the sessions. I will make sure the directions are clear to my facility and sometimes will arrange to meet them to show them around before we even have a session booked in. I am always explicit with clients that I am also autistic. I have found that this knowledge can help to remove barriers both in comfort and communication, as there is an awareness that I also know how it feels to be inherently different in this world. When a client arrives, we will have a check-in together as to how they are feeling coming today and give some time for them to take in the space, to observe any changes, and to begin to arrive in the shared space together. Although I have seats available, I have found that usually this process takes place standing. This may be for a couple of reasons. Autistic people are often task focused, so transitional moments can feel tricky for us; we like to know what the expectation is of us at any given moment. I manage this need by having previously talked through what we will do when they arrive, and again as soon as they arrive, I go through the steps we will take once more to remove the uncertainty. The second reason is we like to stim! Stimming is the word used for repetitive rhythmical movement, which we do in order to regulate ourselves. This may be done when we are feeling anxious, when we are in stillness in order to meet our proprioception (the sense of where we are in space) needs, and also when we experience joy. I have found that although clients do sometimes like to sit, usually this is after a period of movement which allows for various stimming to take place. This is something I also discuss with clients as stimming is very much not accepted generally in neurotypical spaces. I am explicit with clients that however they need to move is okay, and I also share with them that I will also likely have times that I stim. For me, I have developed stims that are less obvious, so I rub my fingers, squeeze my hands, suck my tongue, tense certain muscles rhythmically. Some clients are able to hide these stims and others have either stopped hiding them or have never hidden them so they may also look like rocking, spinning, moving arms in rhythm, or could also be stimming with verbal sounds or words. If clients use verbal stims, then this is something we also discuss with regard to safety around the herd.

Once we have both arrived in the space together and gone through safety protocols, we might enter the field. I choose to work with my herd at liberty in their own space. Liberty for me means that they have the choice to move wherever they want to, at any given time, and have full access to different forage and their herd mates. We are very much entering their space, and this is something I feel important to remember, and I usually spend time exploring this with clients as we begin the work. I have found this shows up regularly as I will often have clients describe that the herd seem happy and that they do not want to disturb them. This has led to some interesting work around what signs might the horses give if they are happy to be approached, how might they let us know if they don't want us to approach. In turn this has often led to exploration around how the client shows their happiness, and how this can be misread. For many autistic people, our faces do not always match our internal feelings. We might be feeling joy, but our faces look like we are angry or upset. This is extremely difficult as the neurotypical expectation is that the emotion and the face will match. This gets even more complicated for us if a neurotypical person tells us that they are happy, even if their face might look unhappy, and we will take them at their word. This can lead to all kinds of confusion and upset. Autistic people will generally take what you are saying as being the truth. So, if you say one thing, but really mean another this can be missed. Being explicit is highly valued by us. Working with horses is an excellent space to explore this as horses will be very explicit with how they are feeling. I really enjoy working at liberty as it allows the horses to demonstrate this so well. I have had some beautiful experiences when clients have built up relationships with the herd and can trust that they are able to read their language, to know when they want to be left alone and when there is an invitation to connect.

Witnessing a client move from sharing space and figuring out communication with the herd to a place of deep connection in their relationship so that each understands the other is a truly moving experience. This can allow autistic clients to begin to explore what it can feel like when they are fully understood, when they do not have to wonder whether they are being understood properly, or whether they are understanding fully. This can be a whole new experience for many autistic people. Something which can often show up is the need to share a lot of information. This can be due to many reasons, anxiety included; however, I have experienced it often due to having a lifetime of not being understood. I know for myself that there is always a fear in interactions, that I might not be able to convey exactly what I am hoping to, that I will miss, unknowingly, a vital bit of information that the other person will need to truly get the picture of what I am sharing. To be honest, it is exhausting and drives me a bit mad. It takes a lot of energy to pass on the information and hold the anxiety around the other person/people misunderstanding. For many autistic people, we have learned the hard way that sharing all the details of an experience is imperative to avoid misunderstanding.

It is worth noting here that many of us autists experience the world in a deeply felt way, in a way that is impossible for words to contain. This makes it extra challenging to try to communicate our experience when words just feel so... well, bland. For this reason, with many of my clients, we won't use words in the same way; we might use gestures, or colours, or sounds to show our feelings or what we want to express. I work in an intuitive way: I experience the world in this way, and it's heightened when I am in a space with horses and clients. This can allow me to really feel the client and then to share what I am experiencing with them verbally. I have found this to be something which many neurotypical people are unable to understand, instead assuming it to be a bad thing without realising that I can no more stop it than I can will myself to stop breathing. I don't just experience this with clients but at all times with everything. It is a lot ,but it also can be wonderful.

Something which I find autistic clients particularly good at is describing the here and now—the noticing of what is going on around them. This can be a positive thing, but also something which can turn into an overwhelming moment. When I say we notice everything, I mean everything. Context is vital, so instead of saying "What do you notice right now?" I might instead ask "What do you notice between Toby and Dale right now?" If I ask the former, then my client might feel they need to list everything that they are noticing (think zooming out into everything that is going on in the environment in that moment, every movement of every leaf or blade of grass), and that will take a long time and a lot of effort. Instead, bringing context into it allows my client to know what I am specifically asking in a very clear way. In the same way, when I ask a client "how are you?" it is often followed by a shared laugh, a shorthand almost of acknowledging that for many autistic people (myself included) asking a question like this without context feels meaningless but also often anxiety inducing: What do they actually want to know? How should I respond to this? The question of "What are you feeling in your body right now?" is a brilliant one, and The HERD Model™ is well suited in this way to bring both context and explicit language to what it is we are asking clients. What is worth noting is that many autistic clients may not know what it is they are feeling in their bodies, whether it be physical sensations or emotions. Many autistic people have alexithymia (which derived from the Greek literally means "no words for emotions"), meaning that they may not be able to tell you in that moment exactly what their experience is. This may be due to having too much or too little sensory input at that moment, making it difficult to make those connections and requiring more time to process. Or it may be that words are not adequate to describe their experience (going back to what I mentioned earlier of finding different ways in order to communicate an experience). I have found that once I have been working with an individual client for some time, we build our own ways of communicating, which allows for sharing of these emotions in a way that the clients feel they are being seen and understood. The dance that happens as clients explore and learn to relate with the herd is also happening simultaneously between myself and the client. All these interrelationships are bouncing off one another and creating, what to me, feels like a beautiful interwoven relational landscape.

As I mentioned earlier, routine, predictability, and transitions are important for autistic people. This is something which I have also found important with regard to coming to the end of a session with my clients. Rather than a gradual pull back from the depth of the work and easing into an ending where the client might choose how they want to say goodbye to the herd or space, I have found that ending sessions with autistic clients is more abrupt in some ways. Instead of going into a space of speaking about what they might be doing for the rest of the day, or other chit chat (which generally we autistic people hate), most clients I have worked with prefer to be "in session" then be "out of session", avoiding the transitory, potentially unpredictable, space of the in-between. This is something that can be explored with individual clients as to their preference, but something which I have found as a commonality in the work. For some clients we will speak about a known passion for them (often termed by others as a "special interest", but I intentionally do not use that term as it can be felt as being patronising in the autistic community), bringing them from the depth of the session into a regulated space where they feel more comfortable; this can help them prepare to come back into the rest of the world away from the field.

Working with autistic clients as an autistic person is a gift. Each time I work with a client and see them bringing more of themselves and being as they are, I find I am also showing up even more as I am. The safe space of being with someone who has faced similar social challenges and navigated living as a neurodivergent person in a neurotypical world is precious and allows us a space of acceptance in a way we may not have ever experienced before. In the same way, experiencing our horses accepting us into their spaces as we are, in all our parts, allows us to begin to accept these parts of us, too. My personal experience with The HERD Institute, and particularly with Veronica, has enhanced this safe space for me to also be seen as a professional in this space and feel valued—not despite but because of being autistic.

Part V

A Million Dreams

Chapter 31

The Inclusive HERD™

As part of our efforts to increase diversity, equity, and inclusion, I have been actively campaigning to change the landscape of our equine-facilitated industry through the message that collaboration is inclusion. I have sought out opportunities for collaboration from outside of the HERD community with other training providers and leaders within the equine-facilitated space with the intention of highlighting growth through support rather than competition. I truly believe that it is possible to shift the culture within our industry to work from a place of abundance rather than scarcity, that there are many ways of partnering with horses to facilitate healing and growth for both horses and humans, and that collaboration does not mean that everyone must agree. Indeed, it is by fostering diversity of theory, methodology, practice, and embodied experiences that will allow us to thrive as a community with the shared goal of increasing access to services for those in need.

Coming together in community with all our different approaches is the essence of diversity. Perhaps I'm being too naïve, optimistic, and idealistic, but I would much rather move forward with hope and risk being disappointed than become immobile through fear of the unknown. I believe in dreaming big and supporting others to do the same. As Marianne Williamson says, "As we let our own light shine, we unconsciously give other people permission to do the same. As we are liberated from our own fear, our presence automatically liberates others."[1]

I was recently invited to be on a panel discussion hosted by the Horses and Humans Research Foundation (HHRF) to discuss the future of research within the equine-assisted services industry. My fellow panelists included Bettina Shultz Jobe, co-founder of The Natural Lifemanship Institute, and Kathy Millbeck from E3A, both organizations

---

[1] Williamson, M. (2009). *A return to love: Reflections on the principles of a course in miracles.* HarperCollins.

that would be deemed within a capitalist framework as "competitors" in the market of equine-facilitated training providers. I hadn't met Kathy prior to this webinar, but Bettina and I have connected over the years and presented at each of our respective organizational virtual conferences and summits. We've also appeared on panels together for other events, such as the one HHRF was hosting on this occasion.

The panel discussion began in the usual way of each panelist introducing themselves and their organizations, highlighting the differences and similarities of our programs. I was very aware that I was the only person of color on the panel, and from what I could see on screen, I was one of only three people of color that were in attendance. While this is not unusual or surprising in this space, it is always something that I am attuned to.

During a segment of the discussion on the importance of designing research that could provide "legitimacy" to our field (i.e., to meet the criteria of empirical research privileged by the medical model), I was struck by how easy it would be to fall into the trap of supporting the status quo that we are collectively challenging. A question from an audience member solidified this sense of foreboding for me when they asked if part of the problem of designing empirical research was the lack of standardization in our methods of working. They suggested that if there weren't so many training providers, all approaching the work in different ways, the industry might have a better chance of creating standardized protocols for practitioners to follow; a step-by-step, replicable, generalizable method of working that could be applied to all sessions, which could then translate into quantitative research criteria and measurable outcomes.

I felt sick to my stomach at this suggestion. The idea that a one size fits all approach is both necessary and possible contradicts everything that I believe in. Granted, I have no context of the individual who asked this question—I have no idea if this was a researcher, equine- facilitated practitioner, or both, or neither—but the gut punch I felt was an immediate, embodied knowing that this was someone who doesn't understand or value the importance of diversity. And when there is a lack of awareness of why diversity of thought, methodologies, and practices is necessary within a predominantly white space, you can bet your life on there being a paucity of cultural awareness and competency as well. It is precisely because of these types of experiences, that we need to keep focusing on increasing diversity, equity, and inclusion.

Over the years, I have offered clinical consultation sessions to equine-facilitated practitioners who are trained in other modalities and want to incorporate more cultural awareness into their sessions. During one such consultation, a licensed mental health practitioner described how she had struggled to engage with a young client, an eight-year-old black boy who was experiencing panic attacks. He had recently witnessed his father being arrested on drug charges, which had subsequently been dropped after a proven case of misidentity. While this practitioner had attended numerous diversity and cultural competency training workshops, she had also previously worked within law enforcement and had family members who were deeply entrenched in police culture. She took great pride in her family's years of service and was frustrated by recent calls to defund the police and "paint them as public enemy number 1." In our consultation session, she relayed how she didn't feel she was able to build a rapport with this boy, however hard she had tried to put him at ease. I asked her what putting him at ease meant. Her answer astounded me.

She said that she believed that her client had absorbed some messaging from his mother that may have exacerbated his anxiety; he'd shared with her how he felt he had to always be on his best behavior, and how he was constantly feeling like he might do something wrong and get hurt. He specifically mentioned his fear about being chased by police. Her response to his very real fears was to persuade him that this was unlikely, and "tried to create warmer feelings toward the police and let him know that they are there to help people, not hurt them." Her intention was to alleviate his anxiety and help him feel safe. When the boy told his mother what she'd said, she immediately terminated her son's therapy with the practitioner. This prompted her to seek a consultation with me to understand what motivated her client's mother to do that.

Despite being in circles that openly discussed the impact of social injustice and racial inequality, this practitioner had responded to a young Black child by unintentionally gaslighting his feelings. Racial socialization—the process by which children absorb behaviors, values, and perceptions about the society they exist in—is an integral part of the formation of racial identity and affinity. For Black families, in particular, part of this process is what is commonly referred to as "The Talk": the conversations that parents of Black youth have with their children about how to behave in the presence of law enforcement. To be unaware of this aspect of Black living highlights a lack of cultural attunement. To dismiss, challenge, and ignore that this is part of living as a Black individual in the United States exemplifies cultural incompetence.

While I was encouraged that this practitioner felt humble enough to seek a consultation to understand why her client's mother reacted that way, I was also unnerved by the reality of how much education was needed for those helping vulnerable populations. We don't know what we don't know. A fish doesn't know what water is. This was the impetus for creating the Inclusive HERD™.

Program Development

In 2022, we launched our Inclusive HERD™ program, designed specifically for mental health practitioners, educators, and coaches wanting to deepen their own understanding of diversity, equity, and inclusion. While the program was not aimed at folks within the equine-facilitated industry with horse experience, our initial workshops also included equine specialists who are working within this space, which offered us some valuable feedback for facilitating discussions based on different levels of horse experience and approaches to being with horses. In partnership with the University of Arizona, we are also in the process of designing research protocols to investigate the impact of centering diversity, equity, and inclusion in our programs and The Inclusive HERD™ workshops.

The goal of The Inclusive HERD™ program is to create more spaces where critical conversations about diversity, equity, and inclusion can be held. While The Inclusive HERD™ program incorporates the fundamentals of The HERD Model™ by working in the here and now, what and how, and I–thou, it was born from intersectional perspectives. My colleagues Elizabeth McCorvey, Alison McCabe, Kate Ford, and Sarah Morehouse all provided feedback on a curriculum that we hope will deepen conversations about diversity, equity, and inclusion, challenge the status quo, change the way we interact, and create a more inclusive way of working with those we serve. Elizabeth and I deliberately invited folks to the team who identify as cisgender, heterosexual, white, women for a couple of reasons: a) we needed strong allies in this work so that the emotional burden of these conversations didn't rest solely on marginalized folks, and b) we had enough experience working within the DEI minefield to know that sometimes people need to hear from those they can identify with in order for learning to occur.

We're also aware that there are different levels of understanding coming into the work. Our positionality and intersectionality—that is, our individual perspectives, experiences, and relationships to being a part of majority groups or not, shape our understanding of differences. I hold non-marginalized and privileged positions of being able-bodied, cisgender, well-educated, and middle-class, and undoubtedly have implicit biases that I am unaware of. While I may be more attuned to some issues of racial inequalities, I don't have the lived experiences of someone who identifies as transgender, and I cannot assume that my experience of being Asian is the same as Elizabeth's experience of being Black in America. By embracing our intersectionalities, we can weave together a more solid framework for these discussions. There is always more work to be done to unearth our biases. As part of The Inclusive HERD curriculum, we introduce a way of approaching conversations by first recognizing our level of engagement with a specific marginalized identity.

The Levels of Engagement Scale (See Figure 2) can be used as a self-assessment tool for different aspects of our identity. I encourage you all to take a look at the scale and consider where you might fall in your levels of engagement for your own identities of sex, gender, race, class, physical ability, etc. As you go through the exercise, remember to utilize the BRAVER process to support you.

The pilot run of The Inclusive HERD workshops provided rich examples and confirmation of how even when we are well intentioned in our quest to stand against bigotry, hate, and systemic inequalities, we are all still products of the system we exist within. One of the most powerful moments during a workshop attended by equine-facilitated practitioners highlighted the differences in our understanding of emotional safety.

I had chosen to work with a diverse herd that day, consisting of a quarter horse, a mule, a Clydesdale, and a miniature horse. The herd was familiar with one another and regularly turned out together, so I was surprised to witness during our herd observation session how much antagonistic behavior was showing up. The participants had interpreted the herd behavior in different ways; the mini was protecting the Clydesdale by running in circles around him; the mule was irritated by the mini and kicked out at him; the quarter horse was old and grumpy and had turned her back on everyone, positioning herself as far away as possible. I asked the group about what power dynamics were at play, how it resonated with them, and what their gut reactions were to one another's interpretations of what they were witnessing.

"I don't think that the mini is protecting the big guy at all," said one participant. "I think he's bullying him to stay in that corner and restricting his movement," she continued. "It's interesting how we all see things so differently, isn't it? I guess it depends on our own experiences, right?"

We had landed on one of the core learning objectives of The Inclusive HERD program: to understand our positionalities within the world we live in. The conversation continued as group members shared more of their experiences.

"I didn't like it when you said that the mare was old and grumpy. I like my own space and tend to be more introverted, so I keep to myself a lot of the time, but that doesn't mean I'm being grumpy" said one participant. "I think she's just protecting herself," she continued. I asked her what protecting herself might look like in this group. "Maybe not saying what I really want to say in case I get it wrong?" she said. Others in the group nodded. "I see a few people nodding. What does that mean to you in the context of our work on inclusion?" I asked. She paused for a moment before saying, "I think it means that some of us don't feel entirely safe."

As we processed what it felt like for her to say this aloud, and for the group to hear her name what had previously not been named, I noticed that the herd had begun to settle into the space and were all now standing quietly grazing in the pasture in front of us. It felt to me like something had shifted in the energy of the group, a collective exhale of acknowledgment with what had just been shared.

I brought the group's attention back to the horses and asked if they were ready to enter into the pasture to spend some time with them. A few people eagerly nodded their heads and began to walk toward the gate. "I feel fine. I mean, we're all horse people, right?" one of them said.

"If I could ask you to just slow down for a moment please," I called after them. "I want to check that everyone is ready," I said, turning back to the rest of the group members who had yet moved. "How do the rest of you feel about entering their space?"

"I'm not sure. I mean, I work with horses but I'm relatively new to them compared to quite a few of you, so I'm not sure I would even call myself a horse person yet!" she laughed. "I'm with you. I'm not new to horses, but I don't know *these* ones. They were quite rambunctious just now, so I'm not sure if I feel ready to join them." said another member of the group. "How safe do you all feel right now?" I asked.

This seemingly simple interaction with the herd opened the door for a deeply profound conversation between group members about how many assumptions we might make for others about what feels "safe" (both physically and emotionally). And that just because it feels safe from one person's perspective, doesn't mean that it's safe for another. Tying this into the context of diversity, equity, and inclusion, participants were able to translate this to majority spaces that marginalized folks inhabit, which may not feel safe, *even if those in the majority hold the intention of safety.*

Through this interaction, we were able to introduce the levels of engagement in a way that helped participants understand the complexities of our social identities on a more embodied level. The biggest takeaway for participants from the workshop was the importance of considering (and their willingness to consider) diversity, equity, and inclusion conversations from a different perspective, because what feels true to one person may not to another. It is precisely this willingness, capacity, and commitment to embrace differences that is at the heart of creating a sense of belonging and inclusion at The HERD.

Table 1. Levels of Engagement
©Lac & Ford, 2022

LEVEL 1

- AWARE OF DIVERSITY, EQUITY, AND INCLUSION WORK BUT UNSURE IF IT'S SOMETHING I NEED TO ENGAGE WITH
- I FEEL VERY UNCOMFORTABLE HAVING CONVERSATIONS ABOUT DEI

LEVEL 2

- DESIRE TO LEARN ABOUT IMPLICIT BIAS, PRIVILEGE, AND POWER
- WOULD LIKE TO LEARN ABOUT STEPS TO TAKE TO INCREASE UNDERSTANDING BUT HAVEN'T STARTED WITH ANYTHING CONCRETE
- I FEEL UNCOMFORTABLE HAVING CONVERSATIONS ABOUT DEI

LEVEL 3

- MOTIVATED TO UNDERSTAND MY OWN BIASES AND PRIVILEGE
- ACTIVELY READING INTRODUCTORY BOOKS ON THE SUBJECT
- DESIRE TO ENGAGE WITH OTHERS WHO WANT TO DISMANTLE SYSTEMS OF OPPRESSION
- FEEL UNCOMFORTABLE SOMETIMES WHEN WORKING ON THESE TOPICS BUT ABLE TO SIT WITH DISCOMFORT

LEVEL 4

- COMMITTED TO CONTINUOUS LEARNING ABOUT OWN BIASES AND FEEL SUPPORTED TO ENGAGE IN CONVERSATIONS
- ACTIVELY SEEK BOOKS, WORKSHOPS, AND/OR CONVERSATIONS ON DEI
- ACTIVELY LEARNING HOW TO BE AN ALLY TO VARIOUS MARGINALIZED COMMUNITIES
- ACTIVELY LOOK FOR OPPORTUNITIES TO CHALLENGE SYSTEMS OF OPPRESSION, PARTICULARLY WHEN HOLDING A MAJORITY POSITION
- MOSTLY FEEL COMFORTABLE TALKING ABOUT DEI
- FEEL EQUIPPED WITH STRATEGIES AND SUPPORT FOR MANAGING ANY DISCOMFORT I MAY HAVE
- BELONG TO GROUPS/COMMUNITIES DOING THE WORK IN MY COMMUNITY AS WE COLLECTIVELY HOLD EACH OTHER UP IN THIS WORK

Chapter 32

Diversifying The HERD

I've often been called a dreamer, an idealist, and an optimist. The implications of these terms are that I'm being unrealistic and lacking in pragmatism. The privileges that I have been afforded in my life in terms of my education and relative economic stability mean that I possess the internal resources to hold an abundance of hope: hope for a more equitable, sustainable, and inclusive world; hope for increased accessibility to services for those who need them most; and hope for those who are often dismissed or invisible to become visible, loud, and proud. Hope is necessary for sustainable change.

Within our organization, a tipping point for change occurred during the global pandemic in the aftermath of George Floyd's murder. We had already been working toward aligning our student intake process, curricula, mentoring, and clinical supervision with our organizational mission, vision, and values. We wanted to ensure that students from marginalized populations felt seen and heard, so that they could lean into their training process bravely and authentically. We began with assessing our marketing materials, hiring a consultant to redesign our website to be reflective of who we are as a community. We wanted prospective students from marginalized spaces to know that they would not only be welcome in this space, but that we are actively looking for them to join us.

We assessed our student intake process with the aim of declaring, front and center, that our organization prioritizes diversity, equity, and inclusion. We introduced our Commitment of Belonging as part of the intake process, which outlines what it means to be part of the HERD community, emphasizing the importance of self-awareness, reflection, and accountability in conversations. We want applicants to understand that they are stepping into an environment where we actively engage in these crucial dialogues as part of the training, and in choosing to be a HERD member, they are also stepping into a space where they are expected to stand alongside marginalized populations. Applicants do not progress through to the interview or the next stage of the process until they have acknowledged that they have read the document.

We also hosted and led several virtual summits specifically to address diversity, equity, and inclusion. Our first Diversifying The HERD virtual summit in 2021 featured Black, Indigenous, and practitioners of color already working within the equine-facilitated field. We followed this with our Pride in The HERD virtual summit a few months later, with LGBTQIA practitioners taking the lead in presentations and discussions. We have continued to host and lead these important conversations. With each gathering, we have helped to support marginalized practitioners in their communities by shining a light on their work, acknowledging that there is much that we can learn from them, and providing a space for connection and community.

We are living in interesting times. The endemic nature of COVID created so much uncertainty and has taken its toll on many of us working in the helping professions. When my dear friend and colleague Elizabeth McCorvey, and I first talked about creating a summit that centered on the work and experiences of marginalized folks, our motivation came from constantly seeing a lack of representation in this space. All those conferences and summits that we'd attended where we were often the only people of color and where speaker lineups were a sea of white faces. If you're a person of color, I'm sure this will resonate. For years I've silently asked questions like, "Isn't it obvious that there's a lack of diversity in our field?" When I look around me at conferences, clinics, or workshops, I know I'm not imagining things when I'm the only person of color. As a presenter at conference lineups, I'm often the only person of color in the mix. But am I the only person that can see that? Do the other people in the group notice that? And if they do, is it okay for them that that's the case? I mean, whose responsibility is it to name the elephant in the room?

There are so many nuanced aspects of "simply" acknowledging that there is an issue. Because once we've named it, then what? Do we spring into action to unearth the reasons why this problem exists? How deep do we dig? More important, who is the "we" that might do this? Elizabeth and I knew that there are a ton of practitioners of color, LGBTQIA folks, and other historically marginalized individuals in the field who are doing some incredible work in their communities. We wanted to increase representation, encourage a new generation of practitioners to enter the field, and actively increase diversity, equity, and inclusion.

The good news is that we don't necessarily have to reinvent the wheel either. There's plenty of research and evidence outside of the equine industry that points to systemic inequalities that can shine a light on why things are the way they are. Applying those to our industry, we can easily translate some key lessons: that barriers to access to education and services aren't only financial; that limited resources include time and proximity; that we all have biases that we need to recognize in order for us to tackle systemic issues; and that as someone who grew up in a city, not in a million years did I ever think that I'd end up living on a farm and doing what I do. So I'm sure that a career within the equine industry is not even on the radar of many of the people we want to reach. So how do we engage Black, Indigenous, and youth of color? What additional factors do we need to consider, both for humans and horses when we broaden our access? And, if you want to work with marginalized groups, do you have the cultural competence to do so?

We need to start asking some hard questions because if we keep doing what we've always done, then we'll keep getting the same results. It's that oft-quoted definition of insanity isn't it—doing the same thing but expecting different results? So, if we are to challenge, change, and create programs and organizations to become more inclusive, what do we need to do differently? How do we challenge the status quo? We've been practicing our BRAVER strategy in previous chapters, but how do we take that into the wider world?

As we've already discussed, we know that for many people, talking about diversity, equity, and inclusion is uncomfortable. We also know that we need to have these crucial conversations to find a way forward. Part of being a champion for diversity, equity, and inclusion is about taking a stand to say that we believe that this issue is important, and that we'll fight alongside those who feel marginalized. That's risky and vulnerable to put yourself in a position where you might stand out from others. For organizational leaders who are willing to take that risk, it may result in criticism from their members, staff, and/or potential customers. It's about choosing courage and integrity over comfort and status quo. It's about leading from the heart and not the bottom line and standing strong in the face of resistance. Because, believe me, there will be resistance.

When we started marketing the Pride in The HERD virtual summit, I posted a graphic of all our speakers to one of the many equine-assisted learning forums on Facebook. I was super excited that we were ready to launch and so proud of our team for pulling everything together. I posted about this being the first ever LGBTQIA summit in our field and how we wanted to celebrate achievements. A few minutes later, I got a notification to say that someone had commented on the post. Eagerly, I opened my app to read the comment only to find one word staring back at me. Someone had simply posted the word "why" in response. No question mark, just "Why…"

I felt like I'd been gut-punched. In my excitement, I'd momentarily forgotten that we are still in an uphill battle with many within the equine-facilitated community in our quest for diversity and inclusion. For a second, I felt winded and defeated, and then I was angry and indignant. All in an effort to mask the overwhelming sadness that I felt for those of us who have so often been marginalized in so many ways. And then I did what many of us do in those moments on social media when we feel angry or shamed. I did some Facebook stalking. Okay, I'm not proud of that, but in my defense, I really, really wanted to see who this person was and what had prompted them to post that. Honestly, I think that there was a part of me (that ever-present idealist and optimist in me) that was hoping that maybe they weren't trolling but actually asking "why" out of curiosity. Maybe they thought that this summit wasn't needed because we're now past the point of needing to re-center marginalized folks; maybe they thought it had already been done. But no. What I discovered was that this person is staunchly anti-LGBTQ and also happens to run an equine therapeutic center that offers to "help people reach their full potential." So, I responded in the only way I could by sending a screenshot of the comment to a few of my allies to find support. I also responded to the original post by saying, "Hey, is this an actual question? I'm happy you asked so we can talk about the importance of representation, diversity, equity, and inclusion that's lacking in our field in general. For starters, if your organization's mission is to serve a wide range of participants to reach their full potential, it's necessary to understand their worldview and experiences to meet them where they're at." I didn't get a response.

Michael Kaufmann is the Program Director at Green Chimneys in New York, where diversity and inclusion is woven into the fabric of the organization for both humans and animals, despite the continuous challenges this brings. Their program has camels, peacocks, horses, chickens, owls; you name it, they've found a way to bring the most amazing menagerie of animals into the process of healing with humans. Michael and I have worked together over the years, serving on different committees and boards of directors within the industry, and I deeply value his perspective. In response to my bid for support, his reply was simple and true. He said, "Diversity goes in all directions. At least she's saying it out loud. Many would just think it quietly." This statement absolutely grounded me back into the actuality of why our summit and these conversations are crucial. His response helped to remind me that the purpose of these conversations isn't to position ourselves as right or wrong but to acknowledge that differences exist and that we will disagree. But it's how we disagree while respecting the dignity, worth, and uniqueness of the other that's important.

Cultivating Change

We need to change how we engage with these conversations. For years, I've been cautioned against naming social justice issues within our field, advised not to use such fighting language or to bring politics into the professional environment. I've also been warned that if I speak out, then I'll be in danger of losing potential business. While I know that this guidance comes from a place of love and a desire to protect me from potentially making myself a target for those whose views differ from mine, it also serves as a mechanism of maintaining the status quo. If we don't name it, it can't be real. Clearly, I'm not very good at following advice, and it might even appear as if I'm doing the exact opposite. But let me tell you, this has been years in the making. Years of keeping myself small and not standing up, for fear of standing out. But in the process of taking the leap to speak out, what I've discovered is that there are many others who are willing to hear what needs to be said. Our virtual summits gathered leaders across our industry to engage in some vulnerable, poignant, and brave dialogues to model what it means to courageously step into the unknown. I believe that these collaborations are critical to our industry and represent the beginnings of real, systemic change. There are many other people who are willing to stand alongside us, too—and I am truly grateful for this discovery. Because this means that we are making a difference. We are effecting change.

Now, I'm aware that there may be some of you who are reading this who may still not be entirely on board with the urgency of the need to have these conversations. It may be that you are on the fence and need convincing. I'm going to take the fact that you're still here as a positive sign, and I hope that this book will help to engage you in further conversations with those around you. A journey of a thousand miles begins with a single step, and we are at the beginning of the journey in our industry to create a more inclusive world.

Since the murder of George Floyd in 2020, I've been paying attention to all the organizations that rushed to release statements that declared their commitment to anti-racism and the need to do better in issues of diversity, equity, and inclusion in their organizations. In the beginning, there was this building momentum and a feeling that "this is it...change is finally happening." Now, I'm left wondering how many of those organizations have actually implemented effective change, big or small, within their systems to make the difference their statements intended. I'm not coming from an entirely critical view; much of this is genuine curiosity. I've been involved in many leadership, training, strategy, and governing body environments over the years and know that this work isn't easy, that many ideas die a death by committee, and that there's always resistance to these discussions both within organizations and in the political space.

What I also know is that while the world around me may attempt to minimize my experience as a person of color, I can continue to work toward highlighting these issues by creating more spaces for these dialogues with the courageous souls who are willing to walk alongside me in my protest. Make no mistake; This book is an act of protest, an act of rebellion for me as an organizational leader in Florida. And perhaps that's what it takes to push for change in a systemic way, to transform DEI from an acronym to action.

As I mentioned earlier, many people, particularly earlier in the life of The HERD Institute, warned me about the dangers of centering issues of diversity in our marketing materials. They warned me that if I were to create a space where the issue of cultural competency is baked into everything that we do, I would lose business and not attract the quality and type of students that I wanted into our programs. I'm happy to report that this is 100% inaccurate. But, before I go into that, let's just stop and consider that even with the best of intentions, the systemically privileged and biased vantage point is embedded in those warnings:

1) The assumption is that I want to create a space that's the same as others that already exist. The kind of space where I'll always be in the minority and feel "othered' in some way. A space where things are done the way they're done because that's how they've always been done. Well, that assumption would be inaccurate. I absolutely don't want to do that. I want to create a different kind of space. A space where students and community members feel safe to bring all of who they are and feel a sense of belonging.

2) The second assumption in those warnings is that I should be fearful of losing business from folks whose values don't align with our organization, and for whom the act of centering intentional inclusion is seen as a negative thing. To be clear, I don't hold that fear because I want to work with people whose values align with ours.

3) Third is the assumption that the type of student I might lose by centering the experiences of marginalized folks are the ones I want in our programs. Well, if my aim is to create a space where marginalized folks feel safer and more included, then I'm okay with "losing" potential students who are not aligned with our mission to increase diversity, equity, and inclusion, because their presence would not feel safe for marginalized folks in our community. And I'm not only talking about safety for our students but also for our instructors (and myself), who also come from historically marginalized groups.

4) And finally, and perhaps this is the most insidious implication—that the students I might lose in this process are somehow more qualified or "better than" the ones I would attract by shifting my gaze to look for marginalized individuals. Well, I don't even have words for that one. I mean, I do, but they're not very polite ones.

Within The HERD Institute®, I am incredibly proud of our team's efforts in diversifying our HERD community. Our DEI strategy of creating our Commitment of Belonging, to declare proudly and loudly to everyone interested in our programs the values that we hold as an organization, is now part of our organizational DNA. Our DEI strategy also incorporates an automatic discount to Black, Indigenous, and people of color to honor the reparation owed to historically marginalized groups, and we've offered scholarships to individuals we especially want to support through our programs. While this may seem like a short-term measure, my eye is on the bigger picture in the long term. I see the first step as increasing the diversity within our student population. Step 2 identifies students who show potential as instructors, so that we can also bring more diversity into our faculty team. This bottom-up approach helps us to identify gaps in our DEI strategy, policies, and practices. Getting feedback from our students is especially important in identifying these gaps. A small shift can make a big difference.

A while ago, I got a call from a potential student who was interested in our programs but felt frustrated because our training schedules weren't compatible with her faith. As an Orthodox Jew, she wanted to observe Shabbat, which meant that she wouldn't be able to participate in our weekend certification workshops between sunset on Friday and sunset on Saturday. Clearly, it wouldn't work for her to miss a whole day of training. So, we created an alternative to our traditional Friday through Sunday workshops and offered one mid-week instead.

I also spoke to a student recently who seemed to be struggling to submit her assignments on time. Talking through her progress with our faculty team, I heard a narrative that this was happening because she'd taken on too much and was simply too busy to do the work required. I wanted to check this out with her because I knew through her intake process that she was really committed to doing the work. Turns out that she really struggles with online learning and while she was able to articulate her understanding in spoken form, it's difficult for her to get her thoughts in order in written form. So, we offered her additional support and changed our teaching policies and practices to be better equipped to catch this earlier in the process in the future. In our conversation, this student made a comment about how it felt more natural for her to talk through her ideas and learning, and how she had always struggled at school and been diagnosed with learning difficulties even though she understood the material. I recognized in that moment that we needed to decolonize our programs to support our students. I told this student that, of course, that makes complete sense to me. As a Black woman in America, and a descendant of enslaved people, her history is rooted in the narrative, in learning through story and not the written word. Instead of seeing this as a learning difficulty, I was curious about how we could showcase her strengths. I recognized that if we want to create a more equitable learning environment for our students, we need to reassess how we assess our students.

Since implementing our DEI strategy, our student demographics have shifted from being only 9% Black, Indigenous, and people of color and/or openly LGBTQIA folks to almost 25% in the last 3 years. In one workshop recently, 50% of the group were people of color and/or LGBTQIA. This significant increase represents the undeniable impact of centering diversity, equity, and inclusion in our enrollment strategy, and is a step toward honoring our vision of making our training programs accessible to those who are historically under-served. By offering a safer and more inclusive experience for folks who have traditionally not felt welcomed into this space, we can support practitioners to serve their communities from within their cultural contexts. This is what it means to turn DEI from an acronym into action.

Owning Mistakes

Of course, learning how to dismantle systemic oppression isn't easy. Even with the best of intentions, we'll make mistakes. I was reminded of this last summer when due to unforeseen circumstances, we found ourselves short staffed during our busiest time of year. Leading an organization through a rough patch without putting undue expectations and burdens on staff members who are already working at capacity is a juggling act. I am ever grateful to our team behind the scenes who were willing to step up and be flexible with changes. It's at times like these that I really feel the complexities of running an organization and recognize the importance of communications within our community. And while there will always be bumps in the road, our commitment to our core values of creating an intentionally inclusive learning environment through a lens of cultural humility remains front and center.

Amid our scrambling to find a staffing solution, I was momentarily persuaded to consider outsourcing our requirements offshore. My friends who work in corporate environments encouraged me to explore hiring a virtual assistant through an agency that contracts workers in India and the Philippines. They gave me solid business (i.e., financial) reasons why this would be suitable for my needs while allowing me to get tasks completed, suggesting that I needed someone to fill the gap so why not try this as an interim arrangement. There were so many logical reasons why this was a good idea: cheaper, more efficient, task-focused workers who would be paid an hourly rate above what they would get locally for similar roles. So surely there was no ethical dilemma. "These people are grateful for these jobs and the level of pay, and they work really hard," I was told.

Maybe. Maybe not. Through a business lens, I could absolutely see how this might be beneficial to me. Through an ethical lens, I could not justify this colonial perspective. But I dithered and was persuaded to try it under the guise of no harm, no foul—and I was desperate for help.

After one day, I realized that I had gaslit myself. Every fiber of my being was rejecting the dynamics of the situation, so I put a stop to the process. This was not okay. It did not align with our values as an organization; it did not feel authentic or relational; and I felt I had compromised my core beliefs. The shame that came with this realization was enormous, and yet I am grateful for this experience. Now, I know how easy it can be to choose convenience over actually walking the walk. Now, I know that at times of struggle and moments of desperation, I will make mistakes but will also have the courage to correct them. Now, I know with certainty that my actions speak louder than words and that if I am truly committed to doing the work required to dismantle systems of oppression, I need to pay attention to ways our society condones these systems by couching them in business efficiency. It's also yet another reminder to listen to my gut.

Embodying a Sense of Belonging

Relying on my gut instinct is something that I have been relearning with the help of horses. Watching my herd, I am constantly amazed at how full of ease their existence can be. Despite the constraints of living in captivity and having their lives dictated to by my decisions of how I want them to live, I have been told repeatedly that they seem happy, healthy, and engaged in the work that I invite them into. The time I spend with them allows me to recenter and reminds me that the reason I do what I do is because of how I have reconnected with who I am with their help. Embodying a sense of belonging to my heritage, my community, my friends, my family, and myself is a continuous journey. My horses help me to find my ground. I sometimes wonder where I would be if I hadn't found my way to horses. I wonder if I would be able to stand with my differences and still feel like I belong. What I know is that I am deeply grateful for all the horses I have had the honor of being with in my life. Nahshon Cook says,

> Horses are the light I'm learning to see. When I follow them, I'm able to find heaven in every step. And in every step, I'm being taught how not to be afraid of getting to know the person waiting for me on the inside. His damaged places, his weakness, his wishes, all of it, and dealing with everything I can, as much as I can.[1]

I don't know about you, but this resonates deep in my bones. The feeling of being seen, accepted and found not wanting in the presence of horses brings me to my knees with gratitude.

---

[1] Cook, N. (2022). *Horses see us as we are.* Nova's Books.

In the process of writing this book, I have had moments when I have felt stuck. I've questioned myself repeatedly about the purpose of putting myself out there. I've been advised against opening myself up to criticism. With each of these moments, I have come back to how I can live BRAVER, practice what I preach, and maintain integrity for the values that sustain me. I have sought refuge with those who support me, and I have discovered that I have more spaces where I feel I belong than I ever thought possible. With each realization, I have found myself repeatedly returning to the lyrics of the song, "A Million Dreams" from the movie *The Greatest Showman*.

I resonate deeply with the theme of the song—the process of daydreaming for a better world and the idea that people will make assertions that my dream and vision is crazy, outweighed by the firm belief that we can have a say in designing the kind of world we want to live in—and that it takes a million dreams to make that happen.[2]

I am grateful for our team at The HERD Institute® and to all our community members who have stepped up to dream these dreams with me. This is just the beginning, and the next dream is already emerging, unfolding, and becoming more real, day by day. I can't wait to see where this journey takes us.

---

[2] Pasek, B., & Paul, J. (2017). A million dreams [Recorded by Ziv Zaifman, Hugh Jackman, & Michelle Williams]. In *The Greatest Showman* (Original Motion Picture Soundtrack). Atlantic Records.

Chapter Contributors

Yoshi Babcock came to the United States as an exchange student from Japan in 1997 and continued her education to become a psychologist. She earned a Master's degree in Humanistic Psychology and became a licensed psychologist in 2005. She has extensive experience with neuropsychological testing and conducting psychotherapy with clients of all ages dealing with anxiety, trauma, self-esteem issues, and cultural differences. Yoshi also has experience in working as a clinical research assistant at Tohoku University Graduate School of Medicine, Department of Traditional Asian Medicine in Sendai, Japan. Her strong passion for connecting with horses led her to earn a certification as an Equine-Guided Learning (EGL) coach and facilitator in 2017. She is also trained under The HERD Institute in Equine-Facilitated Psychotherapy.

Dr. Kelsey Dayle John (Navajo) studies equine/human relationships with a focus on how these relationships impact indigenous education and research. She is particularly interested in the social, cultural, and historical narratives of equine/human relations in tribal communities. She is currently a National Academy of Education/Spencer Foundation Postdoctoral Fellow and is working on a book project about equine/human relationships in indigenous methodologies. Previously, Kelsey taught in the Diné Studies department at Navajo Technical University on the Navajo Nation. She completed her Ph.D. in Education at Syracuse University. For her dissertation research, she worked in partnership with the Navajo Nation to document horse knowledges and stories for the development of Navajo education, research, and a community horse conference. She has published in the *American Indian Culture and Research Journal, Humananimalia, Edge Effects,* and several edited volumes including *Decolonizing Animals, Indigenous and Decolonizing Studies in Education,* and *Indigenous Religious Traditions in Five Minutes.* Kelsey is certified in Equine-Facilitated Learning through The HERD Institute. She is an enrolled member of the Navajo Nation, and in her spare time runs with her dogs and trains horses.

Rachael Loucks: Rachael knew she wanted to be able to combine her two greatest passions: education and horses. After much research and schooling, she found the HERD Institute most closely matched her philosophy of teaching and Rachael jumped in with both feet! Having completed both her EFL levels 1 & 2 through The HERD Institute, she stepped up to become an instructor as well. These days, Rachael also enjoys facilitating learning through interactions with horses via her program UP THERE, as well as supporting veterans, active service members, and their families through her non-profit Operation Horses Heal.

Catherine Manakas is a social worker and an attorney. Catherine spent time working for the State of Wisconsin as an Equal Rights Officer, and while she loved the work, did not love the cubicle. Catherine decided she would rather be in a barn. In 2016, she began community organizing around her ideals and is still locally active in that role. In 2018, she began providing horseback riding instruction and loved it, and helped create a local PFLAG chapter (a national LGBTQIA organization that has been in existence since 1973) for her rural community, and still serves as secretary of that organization. In 2019, Catherine obtained an Equine-Facilitated Learning Certificate through The HERD Institute. In the spring of 2020, she moved to Trident Farm, located in Deerfield, WI. Since that time she has worked closely with Trident's owners to make the sport welcoming, inclusive, and accessible while maintaining a competitive edge. In this vein, Catherine is currently in the process of assisting in the creation of Trident Para Showjumping, Inc., a non-profit intended to support disabled people to ride competitively in the hunter–jumper world.

Elizabeth McCorvey, LCSW (she/her) is a psychotherapist and pot-stirrer in Hendersonville, NC. She is a faculty member of The HERD Institute in Florida, where she helps bring psychotherapists and horses together to support the healing process of their clients. She also works with college students at UNC-Asheville, and has a semi-private practice where she sees clients for individual mental health therapy. Elizabeth is a passionate advocate for anti-oppression, equity, and dismantling the mental health industrial complex, and frequently facilitates workshops for therapists on the subject.

Dr. Danielle Mills is the founder of Pony Partnerships CIC, a non-profit organization in Derbyshire, UK. She started in a muddy field with two ponies, a shed, and a portable toilet, and now works alongside seven horses, three donkeys, six goats, three sheep, and a cat, and has a human team of three facilitators and three barn staff. Pony Partnerships predominantly works with children and young people who struggle to engage in mainstream services and strives to offer an inclusive, neurodiversity-affirming, trauma-informed environment where clients can develop feelings of safety that support them to embrace their full selves. Danielle initially trained as an integrative therapist and went on to train in Equine-Facilitated Psychotherapy and Learning (EFP/L) with LEAP Equine. Danielle continued her training through The HERD Institute, where she is now a faculty member and delivers the UK training for EFP/L. Danielle also holds a Masters degree in Pluralistic Counselling & Psychotherapy, and incorporates this approach into her equine work. Danielle has a PhD in nursing studies from the University of Nottingham and works as an associate academic for both the University of Derby and the Institute of Integrative Counselling and Psychotherapy.

Naomi Nyamudoka, MBACP: is the Founder of Be. Herd and Be. Counselling in Perthshire in Scotland. She works with her herd of four: -two mini shetlands she has had since childhood, a cob, and a young fell pony in a magical setting by the river Earn. She is autistic and works with other autistic and otherwise neurodivergent individuals over the age of 16 and those who have experienced trauma, both in her Equine-Facilitated Psychotherapy practice and online. She has a Master's of Art in Philosophy and qualified as a Counsellor and Psychotherapist in 2017, then went on to complete her EFP training with The HERD Institute in 2023. Naomi is passionate about creating space for people to be themselves and works from a neurodivergent- affirming lens with acute awareness of the intersections of minority communities.

About the Author
Veronica Lac, PhD, LPC

Veronica is the Founder and Executive Director of The HERD Institute® which offers training and certification for Equine- Facilitated Psychotherapy and Learning. Veronica is passionate about increasing accessibility and diversity to equine-facilitated services and providers and is committed to fostering collaboration within the field.

With 25 years of experience as a corporate trainer and mental health professional, and as a certified therapeutic riding instructor, Veronica brings an integrated perspective to equine-facilitated work. Her academic background includes a masters in Training and Performance Management, a masters in Gestalt Psychotherapy, and a PhD in Psychology. She is trained in a number of modalities, including a mentorship in Adventures in Awareness with Barbara Rector, a groundbreaking influence in this field. This has allowed her to combine her theoretical understanding with a relational and embodied approach. Veronica is passionate about bringing a cultural competence framework into the equine-facilitated field.

Veronica is the recipient of the 2022 APA Division 32 Camri Harari Early Career Award from the American Psychological Association. This award recognizes outstanding contributions for innovative applications in the field of Humanistic Psychology.

.

www.ingramcontent.com/pod-product-compliance
Lightning Source LLC
Chambersburg PA
CBHW070326270326
41926CB00017B/3785

* 9 7 8 1 9 5 5 7 3 7 3 9 5 *